ROUGH AMUSEMENTS

Published by Bloomsbury, New York and London
Distributed to the trade by Holtzbrinck Publishers

Library of Congress Cataloging-in-Publication Data has been applied for.

ISBN 1–58234–285–7

First U.S. edition 2003

1 3 5 7 9 10 8 6 4 2

Typeset by Palimpsest Book Production Limited,
Polmont, Stirlingshire, Scotland
Printed in the United States of America
by RR Donnelley & Sons, Crawfordsville

ROUGH AMUSEMENTS

The True Story of A'Lelia Walker,
Patroness of the Harlem Renaissance's
Down-Low Culture

An Urban Historical by

BEN NEIHART

BLOOMSBURY

CHAPTER ONE

A police officer's hoarse voice rang out across the sidewalk. "Hello, pretty!"

Glamorous, light-stepping women, some of them stubbled with a few days' growth of beard, approached the Manhattan Casino on Harlem's West 155th Street. It was a February night in 1930, cold again after a lovely, startlingly warm spell of coatless afternoons in the high sixties. Tonight, the Hamilton Lodge No. 710 of the Grand United Order of Odd Fellows, a black social club, had rented the Casino, Harlem's largest dance hall, for its annual drag extravaganza – what was known around town as the Faggots Ball.

A car horn blared, scattering the throngs who crowded the half block in front of the entrance.

"Who do they think *they* are?" screeched an impossibly skinny, tall geisha who walked arm in arm with a teen-age gangster, a blunt boy who kept patting the front of his pants.

Lazily, a dark Lincoln Special pulled up to the curb, its

1

engine humming luxuriously. The chauffeur, in livery costume, hopped out to open the door for A'Lelia Walker, heiress to the immense beauty-products fortune created by her mother.

"Give me one minute," A'Lelia said from her seat. With deliberate slowness she pulled an ermine cape around her shoulders. A luscious deep brown, highlighted with speckles of eggshell white, the cape set off A'Lelia's dark skin. "Step back! Give me some room!" She kicked one long, booted leg out of the car, then the other, and with a couple of deep sighs she was standing at her full six feet.

Immediately, she heard her name, in whispers, in shouts from the crowd. They still knew her, she thought with satisfaction. They haven't forgotten A'Lelia – not yet. Her mother, Madame C. J. Walker, had been a tycoon, a lifestyle icon, a formidable political and cultural presence. Her savvy in marketing hair-care and skin products for black women had made her a very rich woman, the legendary washerwoman turned black millionaire, and she had leveraged her high profile to advocate social change.

But as far as A'Lelia was concerned, let Madame, God rest her soul, keep her business fame. Let Madame's name resonate in history books and museums. And let A'Lelia enjoy all the spoils that success provided, the clothes, cars, estates, and champagne. Like it or not, A'Lelia was the

2

walking advertisement for her mother's brand name, living proof that black women could live like royalty, even in twentieth-century America. Though the effort had just about killed her, A'Lelia had, by living so well, stepped out from her mother's shadow and become her own damned living legend.

"Come on now; it's cold out here," A'Lelia called to the rest of her party, who remained in the car, finishing a bottle of champagne. "I don't like to be alone with all these people around. Hurry up." She turned to go inside.

"Here we come, Lelia. Hold on." A flurry of legs and arms fell out of the Lincoln all at once.

"I'm not waiting," A'Lelia muttered, starting toward the entry.

"We're coming! We're coming!"

The entourage of four followed close on her heels, but just as the group was about to enter the ball, they were cut off by a drove of fleet-footed, pale "girls" in heels who clattered past them into the warm crowded lobby.

"Excuse me!" scolded Mayme White, A'Lelia's constant companion. Her nickname was Abundance, a tribute to her size and ebullience. She wore two dozen gold bracelets up her bare arms and an extravagant mink scarf wrapped around

3

her neck. She carried a long gray-fox coat, whose left arm dragged along the sidewalk behind her. In her other hand, she gripped a leather satchel filled with clinking glass.

"Let it go," murmured A'Lelia, looking nervously around her. She'd always moved about New York without a care, but over the past year or so her sense of security, especially in Harlem, had been shattered. Harlem was blacks, Jews, Latins, and tourists. White gangsters were all over uptown these days, taking over black numbers and liquor franchises. Their guns, their ruthlessness invaded A'Lelia's dreams. If she didn't love New York City so much, she would have moved far away, maybe the West Indies, maybe Palm Beach, maybe Indianapolis, maybe Atlantic City, places she visited regularly for business and pleasure. Yet Manhattan's siren call always drew her home.

Oh, but who was she kidding?

All but one of the drag queens had disappeared into the throngs. Just one beaten-down, old, pale gal lingered. She had to be sixty years old, in a tight black dress and crooked white wig. "I'm sorry, ma'am," she rasped, looking directly at A'Lelia. "Did they bother with any of your clothes? Scuff your lovely shoes?"

"No, we're fine." Mayme stood protectively in front of A'Lelia.

4

"Do I know you?" A'Lelia asked. "Are you a friend of Carlo?"

The old drag smirked. "My name is Jennie June, and no, I am not a friend of Mr. Carl Van Vechten, thank you very much. And no need to introduce yourself. I know who you are." She stepped closer to A'Lelia, rubbing her palms together. "My advice to you is this: Watch your back."

"How dare you!" Mayme shouted. But A'Lelia took her arm as the crowd swallowed Jennie June whole.

"Was that someone I know?" A'Lelia laughed, looking to her entourage for reassurace.

There was a collective shrug: *no telling who Lelia knew.*

A'Lelia let her eyes instinctively rest on the faces of each of the police officers guarding the entrance to the hall; she had a good rapport with several of the men from the West 135th Street Station.

But no, she recognized none of these men standing post at the front doors.

"You okay?" Mayme asked, petting A'Lelia's shoulder.

"Fine. I'm fine. Let's get inside."

The band, electrically amped for maximum sound, drummed out a soft-footed military procession that annoyed A'Lelia. She had a finely tuned sense of soundtrack, and right now she was in the mood for a song with some swing, not this brusque ode to warfare that made you half expect to hear gunfire. Handing her cape to Mayme, she stormed through the lobby in a huff, the picture of chic in a jeweled red turban, a broad-sashed Cossack dress, high Russian boots, and her Tiffany's brooch, which was platinum encrusted with diamonds. She reached the grand staircase and took hold of the gold banister, closing her eyes as her entourage fluttered around her, whispering, laughing, touching her hair. The only man in the bunch, the poet Langston Hughes, her dear genius, took her arm.

"Are we ready for this?" he asked her.

A'Lelia leaned forward to give him a tender kiss on the cheek. "I believe we're ready, m'dear."

"Well then, let's keep rising."

A'Lelia had to stop after the first sweep of steps. A hand on her chest, she pulled in deep wheezing breaths.

"They need some Bessie Smith in here," Langston said.

She smiled, gasped, "The Four Bon Tons would be nice."

"Yes they would."

Slim, dreamy-eyed Langston, with his innocent mien, his clear smile, could have been A'Lelia's loyal nephew, helping her up the stairs. He was so good at being companionable to rich women, walking at their pace, telling a story, listening, laughing, whatever the moment called for. Unflappable Langston, accomplished Langston, Langston the beautiful boy. He had seen his mother mistreated, snickered at behind her back, and he was damned if he'd show the same disrespect to someone else's mother. Of course, it helped to actually *like* the woman; Langston loved Lelia, despite the misgivings of his uptight writerly peers, the aristocratic fools who looked down on the heiress for her decadence, for her roots, for her lack of deep reading in European literature, for her lack of deep reading in the current New Negro literature, for her deep recklessness, for her loud, long, extraordinary parties, which had the audaciousness to actually be fucking fun, not just a bunch of talking and reciting.

One of his white champions, the omnipresent dandy Carl Van Vechten, had already captured – some said caricatured – A'Lelia in his novel *Nigger Heaven*. He had called her "Adora Boniface." It had been a mistake, Langston thought, to transform A'Lelia from the daughter of a tycoon into just another woman who'd married well – but still, Carl had illuminated Walker's softer side, the way she worried about her friends.

Maybe it would take another one of his "friends," his rival, Zora Neale Hurston, to tackle the story of A'Lelia and her mother, to bring drama to the hair and cosmetics business.

Zora had said something to that effect, and God knew she had a flair for drama. Langston had told her it was a good idea, but he knew she would never follow through on it unless someone else coached her. No thank you.

They could all claim A'Lelia. But Langston had a feeling he'd be the only one of the Renaissance writers who'd be at her funeral – hell, he could imagine himself writing a poem for her.

He didn't care if he was taking a risk, just being here at the Faggots Ball as her guest. You come to the Faggots Ball, they say you're a fairy. You spend too much time beside A'Lelia, they say you're a fairy. Hell, some of the most committed faggots in Harlem were ambivalent about being seen here, lest their names be celebrated in tomorrow's gossip columns.

And, of course, his spending so much time with A'Lelia fueled the criticisms of his subject matter. It was too racy. It was much too Negro. Some of his staunchest allies, white and black, were under the mistaken impression that A'Lelia and her high-living gang were an irrelevant sideshow that might undermine the heavy intellectual and spiritual progress the race had made during the Renaissance.

Langston was so tired of sermons.

And, especially, he was so tired of preachers who were wrong.

As much as Langston had, at the start of his career, bowed to W. E. B. DuBois, the undisputed intellectual leader, so busily promoting the Talented Tenth, that elitist, educated cadre of black men and women "who through their knowledge of modern culture could guide the American Negro into a higher civilization,"[1] he had had enough advice about How to Be a New Negro, thank you very much. Langston knew DuBois took some satisfaction in seeing him on A'Lelia's team: by turning his back on DuBois's exacting standards, Langston had proven that he belonged *down there* with the gutter crowd.

Langston's Godmother, the rich white mystic Charlotte Mason, surely wouldn't approve of his attendance either. She paid him $150 each month to be beatific, to be black, to help her build that fucking bridge that stretched from Harlem to Africa, to sit by her feet and teach her his pagan ways. He'd never quite had the heart to admit to dear Godmother that when he last visited Africa the natives took him for a white man, and laughed at his efforts to connect with them.

Okay, he said to himself, whatever it takes, I've got to make a place of my own in this town. Or I've got to leave.

A'Lelia, for her part, had been a Langston Hughes fan even before they met one another in 1926. She had mailed two copies of his first poetry collection to him, with return postage, asking for an autograph. All the hateful Harlem snobs who said she was dumb, or lazy, living off her mother's hard work – they could go to hell. She read poems, books, newspapers, magazines; it was just that she was honest enough to admit that she didn't always *finish* the reading that she started. Yes, she skimmed. But her critics were the fools if they thought every book was worth reading to the bitter end. Life was far too short. And she often had the sneaking suspicion that, despite all their hard work, most of these writers and painters were not destined for immortality.

But she *had* finished Langston's collection; such a sensation, and the poems seemed like songs to her. Lines lingered in her head the way songs did. They made her feel like Langston's brain meshed with hers, like he was listening to her think.

The Weary Blues sold a brisk hundred copies a week during its first months of release. It was an instant critical success, with positive reviews from *The New Republic*, the *New York Times*, and a slew of southern papers. Just about the only negative review came from darling Countee Cullen, the rival Harlem poet whose infatuation with Hughes (the "bronze Adonis," Cullen wrote) had ended their friendship. Cullen didn't care for the book's "strictly Negro themes."

Never love a man . . .[2]

Oh, A'Lelia knew that line was true.

This drag ball, this camp affair, was not Langston's scene – all this homosexual energy, so openly displayed. Forget it. He had been a sailor, he had traveled the world on his own. Yes, he'd had sex with a man. But did Harlem think it knew him? Did an artist have to explain himself? For all they knew, he had hidden offspring around the world, treasures from girls he might have loved in every port. Or maybe he truly had the freakiest ways, and found himself in strange men's arms every night. Frankly, sex was overrated.

But to put your business on display like this, you had to be crazy, you had to think your sex life was the essential, irreducible key to your identity. It was hard enough to make your way as an artist. Your own people stealing from you, jabbing you. But as a sissy man? Out in the open? And black? You'd end up a joke, your books would be banned, the white patronage would dry up.

Not Langston. Not tonight. Not ever. No dress. No loincloth. No kissing in the alcove.

He was here tonight for two reasons.

The first was his writerly curiosity. Who were the pathetic, bedraggled old creatures in immaculate museum-piece gowns?

And the young pretty things, the slender, clean-shaven drags – where were they from? How many of them had he seen dressed as men on his long nights around New York?

And second, he was here for A'Lelia, the woman he'd christened Harlem's "Joy Goddess." He knew the twenties craze for Harlem had run its course. The twenties were over. With the crash of the stock market, jobs were disappearing for everyone, and that meant they were disappearing fastest for black people. A'Lelia was what 1920s Harlem meant to him, to his youth: music, dance, late nights, a mélange of people who actually exerted themselves, whatever their color, to do the hard work of creating a poem or two, a song or two, an ephemeral moment, a party. This was a moment, a chapter in the history books. It didn't embarrass him to think, to *know*, that his poems were the best that the moment had produced. He was already one of the faces. He had worked so hard to make it.

And so had A'Lelia. She was one of the legends, and she had understandably sought out his company.

He didn't know how much longer he'd stay in New York, anyway; California tempted him, and Mexico, too. So he'd take every chance he was offered to be near A'Lelia. You never knew when the legend might die.

*   *   *

For months, A'Lelia had been living on the very edge of her nerves.

The stock market crash, just three months earlier, had been bad enough. She was not like so many of these women who on a whim had speculated in the market. Not like these women the *New York Times* had written about, storming into their broker's office, badgering the manager for a stock quote, and then dissolving into tears when they heard the bad news. Those comical white women. What was it that one of them had whimpered when her broker told her how much she'd lost? "You might at least be a gentleman." Or the ones who bragged about how much money they'd lost, like it was a game or a sign of their self-sufficiency, ten thousand, twenty thousand dollars, mad money.[3] No, A'Lelia was trying to keep a brave face, to bargain with creditors; she was trying to keep the family business, her mother's empire, as well as her own luxurious life, intact, even as sales plummeted and expenses rose.

Even worse than worries about money were her fears for her personal safety, which she blamed on the mobster Dutch Schultz, the white devil who had kidnapped her friend Caspar Holstein a couple of years back, held him for fifty thousand dollars' ransom. Caspar's picture was in the papers every day until, mysteriously, he was set free.

Caspar was an underworld figure himself, king of Harlem's

numbers racket, so at first his troubles hadn't seemed contagious to A'Lelia. Hell, Caspar's business was earning twelve illegal grand a day. He was buying up property all over Harlem. He bribed white politicians with stunning gifts of silver and jewelry. He'd be at the Saratoga races betting twenty, thirty, forty in an afternoon. He was such an obvious target. But afterward, after all the talk had died down, Caspar told her about a list he had seen, a list of rich Harlem blacks, A'Lelia among them, who'd been targeted by Schultz for future kidnappings.

Now A'Lelia felt vulnerable at these big public affairs. Private parties were one thing. You were in a smaller space. You were surrounded by a select crowd. But in a place like the Manhattan Casino, you could forget about safety. What were there, five thousand, six thousand people here tonight? Side doors, alcoves, back rooms, boys slipping in and out for sex. Who could keep track of all these people? It was madness.

In fact, she very well could have turned around and gone home – but here she was, promenading into the hall, exclaiming to friends, hugs and kisses. This decadent gang was her gang; these louche souls were her faithful pals, and it was her intention to celebrate with them. Who else had been so loyal? The sissier the boy, the more she liked him. She certainly couldn't bring herself to disappoint them. She was forty-four years old, a jittery and impatient millionaire, but she could no more bear to hurt people's feelings than have her own feelings hurt. Of course it happened: she hurt them, they hurt her. But when it did, she felt torn up inside, overwhelmed with karmic foreboding. More doom? That was the last thing she needed; hell, she wasn't ready to pass on just yet.

In her private box overlooking the ballroom floor, A'Lelia sank happily into her chair. She was content to stay up here above the crowd. In this comfortable seat, she could watch friends make their way along the dance floor, watch the costumed drag queens perform for her. And she could give her aching feet a rest. These boots were authentic (they'd been imported from Moscow by Wanamaker's), but they pinched her feet terribly. Here she was, living a life of spectacular leisure, yet her feet always seemed to ache. Of course, they supported a big woman. She was tall, six feet in heels, and a solid 190 pounds.

"I used to dance," she told Langston and Mayme wistfully.

"You still dance," Mayme said, popping one of the bottles of good champagne she'd brought along with a half-dozen flutes.

"Not like I used to. Now, Mayme, I'm thirsty."

"Yes, Lelia." Mayme joke-pouted. After passing the filled

flutes to the faithful, she settled into the seat next to Langston. "This has got to be a record crowd, doesn't it? Look at all those pretty girls." She leaned over the railing to peer down at the dance floor.

Langston, bemused, took Mayme's hand and said, "They all wish they were you. Every last one of them."

The Faggots Ball was New York's largest annual gathering of gay people, yet many in the crowd were straight onlookers, some friendly, some curious, some contemptuous. It was an elaborate celebration hosted by a venerable black social club, yet like every cultural institution in Harlem, it drew white tourists with a taste for exotica. Whatever their motives, the bedazzled onlookers had no choice but to stare at the dramatic pageantry on display beneath a massive crystal chandelier and a ceiling painted sky blue.

Some men were simply masqueraders, retaining the Ball's roots as a costume event without a specifically homosexual identity. But even many of their costumes, in the context of a gay dance party, now seemed more iconic, more exaggeratedly masculine. There were huge, muscular men transformed into loincloth-clad tribal warriors, swaggering Apaches in headdress and warpaint; classical gods wearing nothing but a pouch to cover their sex organs; brutal, sworded samurai. It was hard to tell which of the stereotypic uses of costume and gesture were ironic send-ups and which were plain racism. Mostly, the macho costumes were an excuse for men to run around nearly naked, showing off.

The real stars of the evening were the most effeminate girls, the "fairies."

Hundreds of queens had gotten themselves up in drag. They came as Spanish señoritas in black-and-red ruffles, twirling frilly parasols; as trampy showgirls cinched into iridescent silver gowns, bewigged and capped by ostrich-feather headpieces; as kimono-clad geishas, powdered white, with silky straight black hair; as Floradora chorus girls, imported from the London operetta, all upbeat unison, singing and talking as one, and wearing ruffles and velvet and oversize red bonnets; as camp Colonial Dames, those blue-blooded dowagers; as white movie-star divas, Mae West here, Gloria Swanson there, a dozen Greta Garbos. Not a black film diva in sight; in 1930, there were none.

A few black queens dressed as exaggerated minstrel-show Topsys fresh from *Uncle Tom's Cabin*. In ragged dresses and broken shoes, hair knotted wild, they would turn to each other with a delirious, angry edge to their voices and shout, "Law, Missis! This pahtay's fulla white folks!"

*   *   *

Not all the masqueraders unleashed their inner femmes. A tiny clutch of butch lesbians in somber-hued sack suits shuffled behind the drag queens, yielding the spotlight. That androgynous look was not A'Lelia's look. That open lesbianism wasn't her style either, though the rumors were widespread all over Harlem. Sure, A'Lelia had always preferred the intimate attentions of her close girlfriends to those of her three husbands, none of whom she'd lived with for any great stretch of time. Sure, she told a friend that she'd given up on men because they'd proven themselves so untrustworthy. Sure, friends told her the men had married her just for the money, or to cover up their own strange ways. And sure she had found herself at the Clam House, the gay bar on 133rd Street, singing along with Bessie Jackson's number about bull dykers, butch lesbians, in "B.D. Woman's Blues":[4]

Comin' a time, B.D. womens ain't gonna need no men,
The way they treat us is a low-down and dirty sin.

B.D. women, they all done learnt their plan,
They can lay their jive just like a nach'l man.

B.D. women, B.D. women, you know they sure is rough,
They all drink up plenty o' whiskey and they sure will strut their stuff.

Mayme had moved in with A'Lelia the previous year, and Harlem thought of them as a couple, but if A'Lelia was a lesbian, as some historians claim, she took pains to disavow the rumors. She knew – she *knew* – her community would never have forgiven her for going public.

Despite the homosexual trappings of cultural Harlem in the 1920s, the greater black social and intellectual power structure remained steadfast in its official condemnation of this "perversion," with some authorities going so far as to blame same-sex love affairs on the pernicious influence of whites. Although their gossip columns chuckled in a mischievous tone when discussing gay relationships, the news and editorial pages of black newspapers like the *Inter-State Tattler* were aghast, as in an impassioned front-page editorial from February 1929:

We have no quarrel . . . [with the theory] that [some of] those women who are addicted to the habit (for such it is) have been the victims of a condition growing out of certain "pre-natal" influences over which they have no control . . . [but] we are able to assert without fear of contradiction [that] most of the woman who are lady lovers developed the habit either from association with persons who were addicted to the practice or deliberately in search of a substitute for a man . . . Society will never tolerate this practice. Every man who is married must protect his wife against this practice; and every man who has a daughter will oppose this class of perverts to the bitter end. It is certainly a gloomy prospect to contemplate that each of our women folk will, in time . . . take up the habit of falling in love with a woman . . . The most terrible consequences have grown out of women lovers in Harlem. We have seen more than five murders . . . which grew directly out of this practice between a single woman and a married woman.

A'Lelia'd gone through hell some years ago, when she was the rich new girl in town. She had already gotten used to gossip, but this was the story she would not let stand.

It was 1917, and other black folks, neighbors of hers, people she passed on the street and said hello to, had begun to say she was a monster. They said she'd seduced white girls, her house had been raided, she held orgies, her husband was a front, he had freakish ways. Back then, she'd written to the most trusted man in her life, her business manager, Mr. Ransom, and told him this gossip was the most important, most awful thing that had ever happened to her. She hired a private detective, finally, after the talk had spread to downtown, to Brooklyn. It turned out that two houses on her street had been raided. One of her employees, a woman who sold Walker cosmetics, lived in one of the houses. A complete stranger lived in the other.[5]

For months, the anger and anxiety sickened her. Some days it was all she could do to get out of bed; others, she'd feel fine and then it would hit her; she'd double over in pain, fall to her knees and then slowly to the floor, where she'd lie crying.

A'Lelia had blanked out for a moment. The ball had dissolved, and she was alone with her thoughts.

Somewhere, her life had gotten away from her. She had become a symbol. Poor little rich girl. Dumb girl, driving her brilliant mother's business into bankruptcy. Ugly girl, stuck with husbands who wanted her money, not her love, not her company. Gold spigot, opening the flood of champagne and snow and lively music in that monstrous gilded mansion. Striver, surrounding herself with talent, hoping it might rub off on her. Black bull dyker seducing white girls. A'Lelia and her rough amusements.

Nothing but pleasure, baby.

After a second and then a third glass of champagne, A'Lelia's spirits began to rise. It was a sucker's game, this drinking away the blues, but she'd gotten so damn good at it. The colors, smoky lights, glittering costumes, and

21

banging music were like a pageant staged just for her. She was one of the most famous women in this room, and now that her nerves were relaxed, she began to enjoy the attention from the promenading queens below, who stopped and gave performances beneath her box. When one queen dressed like a loose-limbed Marie Antoinette threw her wig onto the floor and began to step into a sassy little turkey trot, A'Lelia got up from her seat and shouted, "Oh, do it!"

"No, you do it!" a voice called to her. "You do it, Lelia."

A'Lelia turned, laughing, to see her friend Blanche Dunn over in the box seats across from hers. "I knew I'd see you," she shouted.

"I'm just back from Paris, honey. Shopping, darling. It was a spectacular time. Hello, Langston, dear."

Langston stood to acknowledge Blanche.

"Come over for a glass of champagne!" A'Lelia called.

"Love to! I'd love to! But later, I'm waiting for my people."

A'Lelia nodded and pulled Langston close, whispering into his cheek, "You think she brought the Swiss consul with her here? Good God!"

"She may have brought his wife, too," Langston murmured. "You see what I see?"

Langston and A'Lelia watched as an elegant pale couple

in formal attire entered Blanche's box and each gave her an extravagant, open-mouthed kiss.

One occurrence best illuminates the way Blanche Dunn operated. The time is a few years before the 1930 Faggots Ball. The place is a swank restaurant south of the color line that divides Harlem from White Manhattan.

The haughty white waitress saunters over to the table of the calmest, best-dressed, most beautiful girl in New York.

"We can't serve you," the waitress says.

The light brown girl, Blanche Dunn, doesn't answer.

"We don't serve blacks."

Barely suppressing a yawn, chic Blanche murmurs, "Oh, I don't blame you. Now show me the menu, please."

Blanche Dunn was West Indian, a tall, light brown teenager who had learned to dress under the watchful eye of a best friend who worked as a seamstress. In no time, she was popping up all over town, hiding her fiercely disciplined need to be seen beneath a languorous, slightly frosty façade. She took powerful men, often white, as lovers, earning her expensive dresses, fox coats, and diamond jewelry.

It was just "a little harmless gold digging," wrote the decadent poet Richard Bruce Nugent, who kept tabs on her rise. "Within a year of moving to New York, Blanche

23

was to be seen at all Broadway first nights, dressed as well and as expensively as any of the paler ladies who vied for such honors, wearing her color as others did their well-known names, and to the same end. It was a common thing to hear people say, 'Oh, everyone was there,' reel off an imposing list of names, finishing often with, 'and that stunning colored girl – you know, the one who always goes to first nights.'"[6]

When she wasn't moving among rich white circles, Blanche made the Hot Cha, an after-hours speakeasy at 132nd Street and Seventh, her court. Like A'Lelia, she'd be attended nightly by the wittiest and most handsome gay men, preferably the London transplants Caska Bonds, a voice trainer; and Harold Jackman, a model and schoolteacher. Carl Van Vechten, the white fop and society author, would always stop by if he knew Blanche was in town, or if Bessie Smith was playing.

"Honeybees and pineapple trees!" he'd shout, rushing over to her table. Smooch. "I thought you were in Paris undertaking a case of the lesbianisms, but here you are!"

You never knew when Blache might breeze through town, but on that February night in 1930 she was in Harlem, watching the drags.

Who knew what time it was when Mayme took A'Lelia by the shoulder and shook her. "There's a man would like to speak with you," she whispered into A'Lelia's ear. "You want me to send him off without you?"

"Which man?" A'Lelia asked.

"That ofay cop back of the box."

"Stay right here, Mayme. Let me go speak to the man."

The man was an off-duty police officer from the station at West 135th Street. He was tall, on the skinny side, and drably serious in a dark wool suit. He smelled of beer and cigar smoke.

"I have some information," he said matter-of-factly.

A'Lelia said nothing.

"I can be on my merry way, if that's your pleasure, ma'am."

"Please don't fuck with me, officer. You know how I value our time together. You know I will make it worth your while."

The officer looked past her.

"What is your information?" A'Lelia asked.

"I've seen the list, ma'am." The cop pulled a pack of cigarettes from his jacket. "I can confirm that it exists."

"Who's on it?"

"Just a few names I recognize. Jack Nail and Watt Terry. Real estate. A lot of it. But of course you already know that. They seem to be second and third."

"And first?"

"Well," he said. "It looks like you're next."

CHAPTER TWO

A'Lelia did not need any more shocks to her system. With high blood pressure, ulcers, and an overstressed immune system that let every passing flu bug attack her, she couldn't have been in worse health. Her mother had died at fifty-two from the ravaging effects of high blood pressure and kidney disease, and A'Lelia seemed to be headed down the same reckless path.

Despite promises to friends, despite the doctor's warning that she wouldn't live to fifty without changing her ways, A'Lelia kept eating, drinking, and playing as if she were still a twentyish new girl in town.

But then none of her closest girlfriends lived differently – smoking, swilling champagne, splurging on lobster, cake, and Russian caviar.

They had actually laughed out loud, reading an editorial from the *Tattler* a couple of years back. A man had written it; he asked

just why our colored girls are so indifferent to athletics . . . With the exception of tennis and basketball, our girls take

27

little interest in things of such a nature . . . Despite the fact that they have been playing tennis on a very large scale for fifteen years or more, not one of our bronze sisters is capable of winning a city championship.[7]

The only exercise A'Lelia got, it seemed, was from cleaning house when the maid was off, or from cooking big spaghetti dinners for a dozen friends. She used to ride horses. She used to dance. But now her feet throbbed with every exertion, so she preferred to stay on her sofa, a drink propped on the pillows beside her, beckoning to friends, Come entertain me.

A'Lelia understood that the spiking pain in her feet, the cold burning ache that spread from deep within her heelbone in crippling, clockwork waves, was not the worst pain that a woman of her class might endure. She was ever so grateful that the pain was not in the pit of her stomach or buried beneath the skull plate, a cancer. But the way her affliction kept bringing her back to silly useless memories of lost love, her first love, John Robinson, down on his knees on their honeymoon night, pleading with her, was more than she could fight off.

"Lelia, I love you," he whimpered, and lay his head gently in her lap.

"My feet hurt," she said coldly. "I can't relax."

His tears dampened her wedding gown. The sight of his arms at his side, limp, those strong shoulders slumped, just about took her eyes out. What was she going to do to this man? Was she going to destroy him?

Her heart turned to Madame Walker.

Is it a curse, Mother?

Is it the price we've paid for success?

Is this the way we are, Mother?

A'Lelia chose one strand of music from the cacophony on the dance floor below, and she allowed it to expand until it had filled up her brain. She stood on her aching feet, staring at the cop who had just confirmed her spot on Dutch Schultz's kidnap list, and all that she allowed, all that she heard, were the flat keys of the piano playing a soft melody, a song she loved, "I'll See You Again."

She hated the sound of her own voice. She could never hit the subtle notes, the ones that reverberated at the end of a line, but she had sung the shit out of that song, she remembered, one rainy, sweet afternoon at the baths down in Hot Springs, Arkansas.

She used to disappear there when the trapdoor opened beneath her. Forty-seven springs flowing from the mountain's southwestern slope, international travelers, gambling nearby so guys like Caspar Holstein wouldn't get too lonesome on their six-week southern rests.

A'Lelia would take long soaks, deep massages, and she'd just sleep for hours on end, the way she never could back home without waking in the middle of the night.

One day, her worries simply disappeared.

She had written a letter to Carlo, told him that she knew her life would be short, she knew her appetites would never recede, but that was fine, she knew that she'd ride out her depressions and be back in New York before too long.

It had been a warm March afternoon, and for no good reason an indelible feeling of calm overcame her as she soaked. She had such a deep acceptance of herself, her naked self, and she imagined her death would not be painful. She'd be comfortable; she'd be loved; she'd die quickly, such a blessing.

The vision made her laugh, so she took it one step further – imagined herself singing at her own funeral, and she hit every one of the hard notes.

The mourners applauded.

A'Lelia snapped out of her reverie and turned to the ofay cop. "I would offer you a glass of champagne, officer," she said, "but I know you'd turn me down."

"Any other night," the cop said. "Any other night. But you're always forgetting to send me an invitation."

"Well, if there's nothing else . . ." A'Lelia turned before she had finished speaking. "Mayme! Pour me another glass, please!"

"I saved you the last of it." Mayme smiled.

"The last?" A'Lelia pouted.

"It was too good," Langston said.

"Hmmm. What would you think if I threw a little party tonight – I'll make some spaghetti, open some red wine, some more bubbly, just a tiny group of us. Just like old times."

Everyone in the box raised their hand, smiling.

"Count me in," Mayme winked. Her bracelets clinked as she let her arm drop.

"Somebody needs to get the word out," A'Lelia said. "Tell the regulars to come to the apartment at two."

CHAPTER THREE

Even in 1930, this Faggots Ball, as it was known, was not the only drag party in town. Men in the Village threw smaller cross-dressing balls; in Harlem, men held intimate, invitation-only drag parties for their friends who were gay, who were in the life. The Harlem parties were hardly Men Only fetes – exuberant women were welcomed by the queens, as audience and foil. But regardless of the neighborhood or the invitation list, these queens were enacting a Manhattan ritual that had crossed over from Europe as early as the 1850s.

It wasn't a love for European culture that made drag balls so acceptable, so legal, so police protected. No, New Yorkers had one group of hard workers to thank for their right to gather in celebration of cross-dressing, and that well-known group was the city's prostitutes, whose popularity had paved the way for all sorts of decadent self-expression.

How did working girls, or "gay girls," as they came to be known, acquire such liberating social power? Well, you have to go back to the early years of the nineteenth century, the

33

period after the Second Great Awakening, when ministers and priests, moral "reformers," and the burgeoning business communities of the great, growing cities of the East Coast began urging Americans to change their wicked ways. Church and merchant class alike wanted an end to that post–Revolutionary War permissiveness, when citizens had enjoyed rather promiscuous, and well-lubricated, social intercourse. The powers that be demanded an end to drinking, consumerism, premarital and extramarital sex, and general carousing – in short, an end to most of the pleasures that American men considered their birthright.

But this moral call to arms didn't stick. In fact, as Timothy Gilfoyle has shown in his indispensable *City of Eros*, the more repressive the "official" morality appeared to become, the looser the day-to-day mores grew. Society was shifting too rapidly beneath the foundation of church and boardroom. For one thing, an avalanche of immigrants and single men from the countryside descended upon New York and other East Coast cities. These young men without families were not likely to remain chaste. At the same time, young men of means were bored by domestic life, and became entranced by the overlapping cults of bachelorhood and the so-called sporting life, which revolved around the "sports" of fighting, gambling, drinking, and fucking.

34

Donald G. Mitchell, an acclaimed nineteenth-century writer, published his most popular book, *Reveries of a Bachelor*, in 1850. This slim volume, which stayed in print well into the twentieth century, documented the mind-set of happily single men in revolt against settling down.

The book starts with an imagined argument among friends, in which the narrator asks: "Shall a man who has been free to chase his fancies over the wide world, without let or hindrance, shut himself up to marriageship, within four walls called home, that are to claim him, his time, his trouble, and his tears, thenceforward forever more, without doubts thick, and thick-coming as smoke?"

Soon the narrator's arguments grow more passionate as he compares his wonderful days of fishing and hunting to his more recent, more dangerous days as prey, "without traps or snares, or any kind of police or constabulary . . . travers[ing] the world, where are swarming, on a moderate computation, some three hundred and odd millions of unmarried women."

Having women chase him is bad enough, but then there's the horrible intimacy of actually being married, when the husband must endure "maiden aunts [who] will come to spend a month or two with their 'dear Peggy,' and want to know every tea-time 'if she isn't a dear love of a wife,'" as well as bratty nephews, soul-deadening in-laws, and cheap uncles.

But the degradation doesn't end with the tragedy of family. There's also the dreaded integration of the wife into the world of work, where "she will annoy you by looking over the stock-list at breakfast time; and mention quite carelessly to your clients that she is interested in such or such a speculation. She will be provokingly silent when you hint to a tradesman that you have not the money by you for his small bill – in short she will tear the life out of you, making you pay in righteous retribution of annoyance, grief, vexation, shame and sickness of heart."

And if that's not enough to chill a bachelor's heart, "Perhaps she is ugly – not noticeable at first; but growing on her, and (what is worse) growing faster on you. You wonder why you didn't see that vulgar nose long ago; and that lip – it is very strange, you think, that you ever thought it pretty. And then – to come to breakfast, with her hair looking as it does, and you not so much as daring to say – 'Peggy, do brush your hair!'"

Bachelors like Mitchell might make you feel less sympathetic toward the single women who can't find a man. Who'd want such a frivolous misogynist; you pity, instead, the whore who's got to sleep with him. But without a husband, single women of limited means were out on their own, fighting to survive.

For young women of the working class, there were few

decent jobs. You could be a maid, a shopgirl, a factory worker, or a wife, but you made terrible wages. Prostitution was the ticket: for women, it was the second-highest-paying job you could have in nineteenth-century New York. First place was held by the smaller pool of women who became madams.

As the culture of whores, madams, and loyal clients flourished, it spilled into the culture at large. Women of the New York aristocracy complained that their respectable husbands preferred the straightforward company of prostitutes to the subtler, cozier life of home and family. Poor women complained that their derelict husbands squandered the family income on whores. A tabloid press grew around the subculture: prostitutes achieved the stature of semitragic heroines, the protagonists of mass-market novels and pseudo-memoirs. With the refinement of publishing technology, entrepreneurial men wrote guidebooks that cataloged the height, weight, and proficiencies of every girl in an established brothel; you could pick up these compendiums at your corner newsstand. At the same time, there was a boom in the printed-erotica business. Often the two forms – guidebook and naughty picture book – neatly coincided. The first such American guidebook, *Prostitution Exposed; Or, A Moral Reform Directory, Laying Bare the Lives, Histories, Residences, Seductions Etc. of the Most Celebrated Courtesans and Ladies of Pleasure of the City of*

New York, written by the pseudonymous Butt Ender in 1839, was illustrated by seminude drawings of voluptuous, bejeweled women half reclining, legs open.

Once the culture had legitimized prostitution by creating consumer guides to its finest practitioners, it wasn't such an enormous step to bring whores out of the whorehouse and into the light. Not just in "their" neighborhoods, where swells could take them for a drink at the local dive, but into the good neighborhoods. As Gilfoyle has discussed in *City of Eros*, the most expedient way to accomplish this transfer of semiprivate sexual behavior into the cultural establishment was under the guise of theater: nudity, titillation, simulated and genuine sex, all of it in public. For the final thirty years of the nineteenth century, with brothels a fully viable and glamorized part of the culture, you had the rise of the "concert saloon," where the entertainers and waitresses supplemented their income by prostitution. Many of the saloons themselves doubled as brothels. They had darkened balconies and secret rooms where the prostitute and her client could go to have sex. When a balcony wasn't "in use," the enterprising actress might lean out over the audience, bare breasted, and solicit a tryst. Drinks, food, a show, and sex – all in the same building. Taken to glamorous extremes, you arrived at the most highly ritualized celebration of whoredom. This was the French Ball.

From 1866 to 1901, the ball was successively housed in three of the city's leading cultural venues: the Academy of Music, the Metropolitan Opera, and Madison Square Garden. A one-hundred-piece orchestra played for a crowd of prostitutes, brokers, and cross-dressing fairies. The French Ball was the place where everyday middle-class folks showed off their sexual fantasies for a crowd. Husbands and wives switched partners at the ball. Fairies and "real men" kissed in the balconies. Prominent business tycoons made love to underage prostitutes. When the ball was held at the Metropolitan Opera, one of New York's most notorious madams sat in the private box that, during the opera season, was reserved for the Astor family. She sat in the box, out of costume, draped in jewels, calmly watching the debauchery that was all around her as great men of the city passed beneath her, tipping their hats and nodding friendly acknowledgment.

No one embodied the moral contradictions of New York in the mid to late 1800s more than Victoria Woodhull. A poor girl from Ohio, Woodhull was an omnivorous intellectual presence in New York: stockbroker; the first female presidential candidate, in 1872; publisher; suffragist; and celebrity defendant in a series of trials for obscenity and libel.

Woodhull believed that public figures had the right to a

private life, yet to prove the hypocrisy of her political enemy, the Reverend Henry Beecher, she published the true account of the reverend's ongoing affair with a married woman (and was bankrupted by the ensuing libel trials). She offered personal hospitality to the New York City prostitutes who crossed her path, yet she wrote that the French Ball, that public celebration of prostitution, was a collision of "three thousand of the best men and four thousand of the worst women in our city."

By gambling that a principled stand could be bolstered by the selective, "fair" revelation of an enemy's moral failings, Woodhull lost years of her life in a fight to regain her beaten reputation. Her opponents, enraged that she had used their tactics against them, had resolved to destroy her. Although she ultimately prevailed in court, New York was never the same for her. She lived out her final years in Worcestershire, England, the wealthy widow of her third husband.

The ascension of the morality police and the prostitute as awe-inspiring celebrity coincided with larger, radical changes in America's social climate.

By the 1870s, troops left the South, so blacks were on their own to fight terrorists like the Ku Klux Klan. Instead of protecting the newly freed slaves, the government sent soldiers to bust up unions. They funneled money to the corporate sector but neglected the public welfare system. The Supreme Court refused to protect blacks from white discrimination in housing and employment. The Court even disliked protecting blacks from murder.

Social Darwinism had reached its apex. For every millionaire who'd existed before the start of the Civil War, there were eighty by the 1890s. Meanwhile, farmers and manual laborers fell deeper into poverty, slum housing deteriorated to new levels of horror, and more children were forced to work.

The codification of social Darwinism emboldened millionaires and their minions in the press and politics and pulpit to declare war on the poor, to blame the poor for their fate. The president of Columbia University declared that "Nature's cure for most social and political diseases is better than man's."

In the 1870s, you had the Reverend Russell Conwell beginning his cross-country lecture tour, declaring, "I say that you ought to get rich, and it is your duty to get rich. There is not a poor person in the United States who was not made so by his own shortcomings, or by the shortcomings of someone else. It is all wrong to be poor, anyhow."

If no one in the government wanted to pay attention to what society as a whole was doing, if laissez-faire ruled in business and military practices, still the natural human instinct for policing, well, it had to express itself somewhere. And family relations were a natural target for meddling.

This was the Gilded Age. Everyone wanted to get rich, get a better house, get a prettier wife – and pay absolutely no attention to the poor. After fighting so hard and suffering such deep blood losses in the Civil War, the American people almost immediately went on a binge of money grubbing and ass grabbing. It was as if the country had a hidden agenda: Let's hurry up and get rid of slavery so we can loot the national bounty. And the national booty.

More money in the hands of more men meant more sex.

During the heyday of the French Ball, several infamous dives took their place in New York history as the first more or less official gay bars. In the mid-1880s, the underworld figure Billy McGlory opened his short-lived saloon, Armory Hall, on Hester Street.

The top-hatted, mustachioed, mercenary McGlory, who'd done time as the leader of the Forty Thieves gang, ran a mean saloon. You had to push through filthy double doors, below the first floor, and make your way down a pitch-black fifty-foot tunnel to the bar and dance floor. With every step you took, the noise of a musical trio – piano, violin, and cornet – blared louder.

The place itself was a drab auditorium, plainly furnished, with an elaborate series of subdivided balconies in which waitresses, full-time prostitutes, and fairies, gay men in full drag, many of whom preferred to live as women, shrilled in high-pitched voices, dancing the cancan, cavorting with customers, and soliciting sex.

The city and the reform-minded press had it in for McGlory, shutting down Armory Hall after just a few years. But by 1892, an even more decadent spot had opened.

The Slide opened at 157 Bleecker Street, on a notorious block where women sat behind drawn shutters, soliciting men through open slats, where grocery stores at dusk converted themselves into whore-friendly dives, where odorous drunks of both sexes staggered from one all-night saloon to the next, looking for wallets to lift.

The Slide was a basement nightclub with a bar up front, tables in the back, and a summer garden. Hundreds of men (but only a handful of women) thronged the place every night.

A reporter from the *New York Press*, which had led the charge against Billy McGlory, was even more aggressive against the Slide, sending an undercover reporter to expose the fairies.

In the January 5, 1892, issue, he wrote:

There were the same steps leading down from the sidewalk which painfully suggest the proverbial "easy descent to

43

hell . . ." The bar was running at full blast and there was a fair sprinkling of bloated, dissipated looking men, some young and some old, who were bandying unspeakable jests with other fastidiously dressed young fellows, whose cheeks were rouged and whose manner suggested the infamy to which they had fallen.

As I entered I was regarded rather suspiciously by the bartender and as I ordered a drink carelessly one of the gaudily bedecked young men minced up to me and lisped, "Aren't you going to buy me something?"

. . . There was a group of men around the bar, and men and women sat at tables at the foot of the raised platform. On this raised dais were half a score of the rouged and powdered men and youths who usually amuse the company with their songs and simpering requests for drinks.

. . . On Sunday night the place was running at full blast and the waiter told me that they sold nearly one hundred bottles of wine on that evening.

"Come in again, sir, in a week, and we'll show you something worth seeing."

A decade later, the Sharon Hotel opened on Third Avenue, near Fourteenth Street. Affectionately known as "Cocksuckers

Hall," the Sharon offered dozens of young male prostitutes for the pleasures of so-called real men. And at the intersection of Twentieth Street and Third Avenue, Billy's Hotel operated on an even larger scale – seventy-five drags working the warren of tiny locked basement closets. These "girls," in blond wigs and minis, wore grooves in the floor on the walk back and forth from the saloon proper.

For every pretty maid, a sport soon appeared, cash in hand.

CHAPTER FOUR

Twenty blocks south of the Faggots Ball, at the Hot Cha, the forbiddingly exclusive speakeasy where Billie Holiday would soon be discovered, glum George Hannah stood slumped next to the piano, letting Meade Lewis carry him through his saddest number, "Freakish Man Blues":

She call me a freakish man – What more was there to do?
Just cause she said I was strange that did not make it true.
I say you mix ink with water, you bound to turn it black.
You run around with "funny" people, you'll get a streak of
    it running up your back.

There was a time when I was alone, my freakish ways
    to treat,
But they're so common now, you get one every day in
    the week.[8]

At a table near the back of the club, three slim gangsters in varying stages of drunkenness argued over the necessity of taking on the black business leaders of Harlem now that the economy was a wreck.

They were midlevel guys associated with Arthur Simon Flegenheimer, who changed his name to the press-friendly Dutch Schultz. Once he learned, in the mid-1920s, that bootlegging was the best way to make significant money, Schultz leveraged his reputation for brutality into a partnership with his boyhood friend Joey Noe. In the late twenties, Schultz committed his first famous kidnapping: the speakeasy owner Joe Rock, who'd made the mistake of balking at the prices Schultz charged for bootleg beer. Schultz's gang blindfolded Rock with a bandage that had been saturated with discharge from a gonorrhea infection and hung him by his thumbs on a silver meat hook. Rock's family paid thirty-five thousand dollars' ransom, but Rock went blind shortly after his release.

Now Dutch's gang was looking to solidify its control on the Harlem nightlife and business communities. They'd already taken on the black bootleggers and gambling kings. The kidnapping of Caspar Holstein, with its attendant press coverage, had sent exactly the message they'd intended. But with the stock crash and depression, Schultz was looking to expand into Harlem real estate, politics, and maybe, just maybe, the hair business.

"Jack Nail and Watt Terry are holdin' a lot of high nothing," one young associate said, cupping a cigarette. "You think this real estate is gonna hold? They were payin' Negro premiums to begin with."

"Girls're still getting their hair done," another associate said.

"Even if you're poor, you don't want the kinks comin' back – now do ya?"

"So Walker's still in play?"

"Fuck yes. I got a cocksucker down the street right now, he's all over her, gonna figure out the right time."

The drunkest gangster rubbed his eyes. "Listen to this! What? What the fuck is this guy singing?"

On stage, George Hannah swayed gently, eyes closed, as, in his high, defeated voice, he sang on:

Had a strange feeling this morning where I've had it all day.

Had a strange feeling this morning, I've had it all day.

I wake up one of these mornings, that feeling will be here to stay.

CHAPTER FIVE

Back at the Faggots Ball, in the corner of the Manhattan Casino that was farthest from the band platform, hidden from view by stacked boxes and wooden ladders tilting against the wall, a form moved from the rear of a dark alcove. You could just barely see a smear of light at first, and then the shape became distinct, shimmering in the night.

First the high piles of white hair. Then the sparkle of beads on an evening gown. Then the face, ravaged by time.

Jennie June, the old drag who'd rasped her warning to A'Lelia Walker on the street in front of the dance hall, stumbled out of the alcove, wiping her mouth with the back of her hand.

Where was she? What time was it?

Oh.

Remembering everything, yet again, she pulled her dress down, smoothing the gathered front, checking for tears in the silk where the brutal young man, in his haste, had gripped her.

Well, everything seemed to be in place, *externally*.

She pulled in a deep breath to see if her lungs, her ribs, had once again survived one of her Jennie June sprees. Forty years and counting. Good God, she'd had a long run in this town.

Now she cupped her hand over her lips and ran her tongue over her teeth, checking whether her upper plate was secure against her gums. Although she had known since she was small that hers was the soul of a girl trapped in a nominally male body, age had taken the pleasure of her femininity away from her. Clicking her teeth, she felt more reptilian than womanly, a lizard losing its fangs after a feeding. You had to adjust your expectations.[9]

It had taken her becoming an old man in her sixties, losing her teeth, to finally understand, to experience how much easier it was to perform fellatio with nothing between your gums and a man's membrum. Back in her prime, the 1890s, half the saloon fairies she knew, the full-time fairies with their Oscar Wilde bangs and their red ties and their narrow narrow shoulders, had gotten their upper teeth replaced with a bridge: you'd slide your teeth out and click drop them in your palm as you fell to your knees. Of course, after a while the saloon fairies became accustomed to going toothless – "Oh, hello, darling," they'd lisp, gliding softly toward you, cheeks painted ocher, nose powdered, lips, outlined blood red, parting in a dark gaping smile.

Jennie, a university graduate with a professional editing job at a top legal-publishing house, had thought herself too high class for such an alteration. What would her uptown peers think of her?

My uptown peers! Oh, dear Jennie, you were such a fool.

The bitter laughter would choke her now, if she let it – the very idea that she'd had a reputation to protect. By the time she'd turned twenty-five, she'd lost her reputation with school, family, church, and state. And yet she'd survived. What else could happen? She had been blackmailed, jailed, beaten, disowned, and raped. Was her murder the only punishment that hadn't befallen her?

If only she were blossoming now, coming into her own in 1930. 1930 was a dreamworld compared to 1895.

She might have become a celebrity. Her memoirs might have had some respect from the literary world rather than making her into a quickly forgotten medical curiosity. Yes, she had written three books about her underworld life.

My time has passed, she thought, looking out on the floor.

I'm part of the past, holding on for dear life.

And these are the new queens of New York, dancing and looking for love.

So many of us. Who could have imagined there were so many of us.

These sparkling lights, this loud band, these celebrities of the theater and art world who sit in the VIP boxes, at the spotlit table reserved for the judges who will decide the awards for Best Costume, Best Makeup, Best Hair, and so on.

Jennie could barely see across the great hall to the judges' platform, but she knew who they were.

Of course there was Carl Van Vechten. Jennie guessed that she should have been flattered, the way A'Lelia Walker asked her, "Are you a friend of Carlo?" As if Jennie were a celebrity, a regular at Gatsbyesque parties. As if a prominent fairy like Carlo lingered in the company of broken-down drags like Jennie.

You'd never see it. Van Vechten was a novelist who aspired in his work and life to the style of fey absurdism that the British novelist Ronald Firbank had popularized in Europe. Carlo was the most effeminate married man Jennie had ever seen. Ridiculously tall and white blond, snaggletoothed, with a lurching walk and a quick superficial wit. A writer for *Vanity Fair*, among other glitzy magazines, he famously wrote a 1923 article for the magazine in which he listed James Joyce, D. H. Lawrence, and Sigmund Freud among the "ten dullest authors." He was in his forties, and still he went to every party that was worth knowing about. He was entrenched with the Arensberg couple, who thought they'd discovered Duchamp, and he had been a force in Mabel Dodge's New York salon, where society, art, political, and literary figures famously met downtown. Van Vechten had championed Harlem's artists, musicians, singers, and poets among influential, curious whites. In a 1925 letter to H. L. Mencken, he had complained about being "a Nordic when you're struggling with Ethiopian psychology." Before he published the self-inflicted succès de scandale *Nigger Heaven*, Van Vechten entertained an idea of himself as the Great American Novelist. He had been celebrated by half the Harlem literati and reviled by the other half; immortalized in the popular song "Go Harlem." He drank to excess, experimented with drugs, stayed up all night, and conducted homosexual affairs out of his wife's hearing. When he let down his tiny guard his speech was florid with sugary baby talk; for instance, a sexy boy was known as an "essbee." Jennie could relate.

Sometimes she thought the only difference between Van Vechten and herself was the ten years that separated them in age. He was a florid sissy, yet he was celebrated in every circle of New York.

On the scale of virility that Jennie June had developed in

55

her youth, Van Vechten was just a few degrees more masculine than Jennie herself.

The other judges were less famous in Harlem. Muriel Draper's lasting fame was as the forbidding mentor to ambitious young homosexuals like Lincoln Kirstein, the cofounder with George Balanchine of American Ballet Theater.

Robert Chanler, the third judge, was known as "Sheriff Bob," and threw parties that rivaled A'Lelia's for their decadence – though the crowds were far whiter. An eccentric Whitney heir, a screen and mural painter, Chanler tranformed rooms into fantasies, explosions of flames, ocean waves, and mythological creatures that only the richest clients could afford.

Each drag on the floor wore a number pinned to her costume, so the judges could keep track of the favorites. The girls would make a special play for attention in front of the boxes where A'Lelia and other society figures held court as the band, led by John C. Smith, whipped the audience into a frenzy. The girls, strutting the runway, demanded the appropriate musical accompaniment to their moment in the spotlight. Hulas, Lindy hops, waltzes, a wailing sax solo.

There was a part of Jennie that wanted to march to the

floor, push those baby girls out of her way, and command the attention of the entire Manhattan Casino.

But no, she thought. To this world, I'm nothing, I'm no one – I never really existed.

Here was the life that used to hide in the dank Bowery slums, block after block of Jennie's favorite Italians, Irish, and Jews. The well-built immigrants, shoved together in close quarters, ripe for one of Jennie's kisses. As the broad-shouldered young men held her in their arms, she'd take their fingers and slowly kiss them, transfixed by their beauty. That was the Bowery in the 1890s.

Now the fairies from every neighborhood in town had converged on Harlem. Jennie supposed it took a powerful woman like A'Lelia to make fairies popular up here. The daughter of power wielded her influence generously, didn't she, front and center, a coterie of sleek young fairies trailing her every step.

Oh God, Jennie was tired, so tired.

Hadn't eaten, hadn't taken her potassium iodide, the fifteen, twenty grains that were like an antidote to the exhausting effects of fellatio. Tomorrow she'd have a fever, she was certain of it. A girl learned from experience. Fever, aching muscles. She'd be sore in the back of her throat, she'd be irritable, forgetful. The seed she took in her mouth, virility she'd just swallowed, was at deep war with her feminine nature. The battle, male versus female, tore her apart.

The man had shoved her against the wall so hard she'd seen an angel out of the corner of her eyes. He'd taken her back in the alcove and when he unbuckled his trousers she saw the gun clipped to his pocket. Another gangster, the kind her friend Phyllis had been so fond of.

"You smell good for an old fairy," he whispered, and pushed, pushed, pushed her head down.

"Thank you," she mumbled, trying not to cry.

But no. She belonged in the shadows. Abandoned tonight by her old friend Angelo Angevine, a fairy she knew from days walking on the Rialto. Angelo, who was known as Phyllis, had started with her own criminal gang in the 1890s. A tough sissy, the leader of a boy gang, tough youths who pickpocketed the Bowery. Phyllis was dried up these days, but some of her boys had grown into the crime life; they knew people in Dutch Schultz's gang. One boy with a perfectly proportioned torso was here tonight, keeping an eye on Harlem, the bootleg trade, the money blacks. He wore a tight suit. He'd been a good soldier in jail, hadn't squealed. Talked about the fairies in jail. Outside on the street, tonight, before the ball, told Jennie right to her face, "These fairies were young. These fairies, God, so pretty you wouldn't even know they were boys. They wanted to be in jail." Then he'd pointed out A'Lelia Walker, the heiress, and told Jennie that there was money to be made off that one. You watch.

A criminal had no qualms confessing to a fairy, because what will the fairy do to him?

Now she leaned back against the wall and let her eyes flutter shut. So quiet. A girl needs to sleep.

Jennie woke up against the wall and screamed. "Don't let them take me there," she sobbed. "Don't push me!"

After a half hour had passed, Jennie looked down and was surprised to see herself in a dress. There was still enough male in her to surprise her.

Sometimes Jennie forgot she was a fairy. Maybe, just maybe, she wouldn't have had to take the transformation so far. Getting herself castrated, for instance – had she really needed that?

Oh, his schoolmates knew what kind of boy he was when they – when they kissed him. He would overarticulate his lips when he was talking, or even when he was listening, getting ready to talk, this unconscious pursing, making kissy-faces, not like a regular girl, either, but like a cartoon, extremely immature girl.

He remembered that he was in high school, walking through town, the woods close, just outside the line of buildings, when this young tough boy with a broad chest and a thick neck passed him on the street and called to him with no malice in his voice, "Hello, Pussy!"

He felt something shift inside him, a rush of pleasure, more, more, say it again. All he wanted was for the boy to come back and call him "Pussy."

Now, as the image of the beautiful boy floated against closed eyelids, Jennie shouted, "Call me Pussy. Call me Baby."

Jennie was startled awake by the force of her own voice, and when she opened her eyes she saw a young black man in spectacles and dark suit open at the neck, smoking hard on a cigarette, approaching her with a smile. The young man – she had forgotten his name, was it Jack? – leaned his face toward Jennie's and said, "Hello, Pussy!" He passed her a glass of water. He had a glass of whiskey and a fresh pack of cigarettes that he seemed intent on smoking one after the next.

"Oh hello, you! I can't tell you how much I worship you. Huge strong hands. Here, hold your hand to mine."

The young man, bemused, held up his hand and opened it, palming Jennie's palm.

"Oh, your hand is so much larger than mine."

"Indeed. But I want to hear about you. You look like you have some stories to tell. I mean, to *tell*."

"Oh my goodness, yes."

"How long have ya been in New York?"

"I moved here in 1891. Summer. I was sixteen. Came for college and missionary work. I was a boy then. Earl. Earl Lind."

The young black man said he was a writer.

"I wrote my books," Jennie June said. "My memoirs. Published, promoted secretly, doctor to doctor, as medical documents, stories of a freak, a sideshow, with bookend commentary by doctors – who tried to explain me to the reader. My sad case. My pathos clinically and coldly dissected. No one knows my books. What do you write?"

"I'm a reporter. I wanna be like Stephen Crane. Tell the true story. I've got some work from the black press. I'm writing a nice article on passing."

"Oh, men passing as women?"

"No. Blacks passing as white."

"Oh. Oh. I would like to read that. Will you be sure to send a copy?"

The young man smiled.

"When I first began to think of publishing my memoris, I took an occasion to make an appointment with Anthony Comstock," Jennie said.

"*The* Comstock?"

"Oh yes."

"You had connections, I take it."

Jennie nodded.

"Go on."

"In the United States the penalty for sodomy was from five to twenty years imprisonment. This penalty was on my mind for the two conferences I had with Comstock because part of his business while alive was that of hunting down fairies and hauling them off to prison. In 1900 I submitted my book to Mr. Comstock in order to ascertain whether it could be circulated without penalty. He was then a post office department inspector, with power to prosecute for shipping 'obscene material' by common carrier. He read a considerable part of the manuscript and stated that he would have destroyed it but for the fact that I impressed him as a person not having any evil intent. Which was a tribute to the mildness of my male persona."

"It's hard to picture you, uh, mild," said the young writer.

Comstock, both Jennie and the young writer knew, was the hypocrite who battled to make birth control and abortion illegal. He wrote lurid narratives about the low life – dive bars, explicit theaters, pool halls. He went "undercover," impersonating an illiterate pauper in search of an abortion for his wife. He had an immense collection of books and photographs he found during raids which he couldn't seem to destroy. He just had to read and reread the worst narratives, as if he were reliving those lurid tales. Fat, bald, with huge walrus whiskers, Comstock was an unknown Civil War veteran who, by sheer force of will, force-fed to Congress the "Comstock Law" on censorship, which passed in 1873, and bombarded the government with slogans such as "Morals – not art and literature!"

For more than forty years, he served as an unpaid, wildly powerful postal inspector, empowered to burst into any post office in the country to impound anything he thought was obscene. Under his leadership, the government burned more than 120 tons of written material.

He was so eager, even medical textbooks stopped discussing contraception.

But he didn't burn Jennie's book, and in fact gave it back to her.

"But he had to have the final word," Jennie rasped to the young writer. She pulled her chin into her neck and let her voice drop: "'These inverts are not fit to live with the rest of mankind. They ought to have branded in their foreheads the word "unclean," and as the lepers of old, they ought to cry "Unclean! Unclean!" as they go about, and instead of the law making twenty years' imprisonment the penalty for their crime, it ought to be imprisonment for life. Are they assaulted and blackmailed? They deserve to be. They are willfully bad, and glory and gloat in their perversion. Their habit is acquired and not inborn. Why propose to have the law against them repealed? If this happened, there would be no way of getting at them. It would be wrong to make life more tolerable for them.'"

"Are you a fairy?" Jennie asked the young reporter.

"I've been known to indulge, but no, I'm not a fairy."

"Do you know the origin of the word?"

The young man shrugged, lit another cigarette.

"The term 'fairy' probably originated on sailing vessels of olden times, when voyages often lasted for months. While the crew was either actively or prospectively suffering acutely from the absence of the female of the species, one of their number would unexpectedly betray an inclination to supply her place. Looked upon as a fairy gift or godsend, such individual would be referred to as 'the fairy.'"

"Damn."

"As a writer, you are naturally more inclined to be a fairy. There is a continuum of masculinity. Do you know it?"

"Um . . . no."

"At the masculine pole stands the warrior, the blue-jacket,

the pugilist, et cetera, and it is only such, the tremendously virile, who possesses no gentle or feminine traits at all, to whom I was ordinarily attracted. Further down the male side of the scale, after the man of adventure and sport, come successively the stevedore and his like, the manual laborer, and the merchant, and still lower, the scholar, which class possesses in general only a comparatively low degree of masculinity and virility. Partaking largely of the feminine type of mind are the male dressmaker and milliner, and the dilettante.'"

"Well, how about that?"

Across the dance floor, Carl Van Vechten shouted, "Tickletoes and pussy willows!" and threw open his arms to greet the beautiful poet Richard Bruce Nugent, who shambled up to him, a plume of pale cigarette smoke around his face.

Jennie watched in disgust and turned back to her young man.

"If I hadn't been a Christian, I would never have found these perfect specimens of man," Jennie said. "When I went to the slums, it was as a missionary."

She accepted the offer of a marijuana cigarette and sat beside the young black man. "It was especially unfortunate that I saw so much of the loose morals . . . The adolescents

65

there attracted me powerfully, and suggestions came into my mind repeatedly to accost them with an indecent purpose. I was also in love with athletic classmates. In the lecture rooms I found it advisable to take a front seat since the sight of an athlete would hypnotize me, making me stare at his form and disregard the lecturer. If one seated himself beside me, shameful thoughts would come into my mind at once. But not only mine. Some of them . . . put their arms around me and you know what they said to me, you know what they called me, they called me 'Child.' I would be so preoccupied that when the professor asked me a question I could hardly answer. I would be thinking of the soft satin-smooth *cuutis in inguine* of the boy beside, which I was sure I would have found *gratissima tactioni, praesertim labiali et linguali,* and I would despair of it being denied to me to touch *on viro* this marvelously fine integument . . ."

"What'd you say?"

"Him . . . in my mouth . . ."

The young man nodded. "So the first night you went out on the town? What happened?" He pulled a notebook from his pocket. "Have there been any articles? On you? Your life? Carl Van Vechten said he might get one of my pieces in *Vanity Fair.*"

"Oh, and where did you meet him?"

The young reporter changed the subject. "I want to hear about your first night on the town. Please."

Jennie ran her palm across her forehead and then along the side of her face. "It was early June in 1892. I had been studying up until the moment I decided that now, finally, was my time. I couldn't bear it one more moment. It was time for my first nocturnal ramble. I put on a cast-off suit which I kept for wear only in my room, placed some coins in a pocket and several bills in a shoe, stuffed a few matches in one pocket and in another a wet sponge, wrapped in paper so as not to dry out, and then carefully went through my clothing a second time to make sure that I had not by oversight left on me some clue to my identity."

"The sponge was for cleaning up, I get that, but the matches – I don't get the matches. And you were a man then. You went out all mannish, did you? You didn't do drag?"

"My darling, life wasn't like today. I could not walk into my dormitory room as a shy young Christian and come out, an hour later, in a gown. Nothing would have pleased me more than to adopt feminine attire on this and my multitudinous subsequent female-impersonation sprees, as some other androgynes are in the habit of doing when going out on similar promenades, but my position in the social organism was much higher than theirs, and the adoption of female apparel would have been attended with too great a risk. The mere wearing of it on the street was grounds for imprisonment. The law was very selective, mind you. It was hard enough to leave the boardinghouse with such a shabby suit. I couldn't be seen in this suit. I crept stealthily out of my room, closing the door softly so as not to attract attention. After listening to make sure that no one was about to ascend the outside steps leading to the street, I opened the outer door and glided out bareheaded, a shabby soft cap crumpled up in my hand because I was ashamed to be seen wearing it by anyone who knew me. Hurriedly crossing to the opposite side of the street, I put on the cap, pulling the tip down over my eyes. Walking a few blocks to a park, I took my house key from my pocket and hid it in the grass, so that it could not be stolen and I thereby rendered unable to let myself in on my return.

"I made my way to the quarter of the city bordering the Hudson River that is given over largely to factories and freight yards and is known as Hell's Kitchen because of the many steam vents. Lonely at night, these blocks, perhaps the most advantageous in the city for highway robbery. I encountered this hulking youth, tall and broad shouldered, with dark hair and eyes, and my full nature just exploded out of me. Suddenly I was Jennie June."

"How'd you come up with the name?"

"I liked the way it sounded. June is the youngest month, you know?"

"And you haven't had to trade it in for something more mature or anything like that?"

"Young man!"

"I'm sorry."

"Apology graciously accepted."

"So how would you come up to a guy?"

"I was possessed, as I told you. I wasn't Earl any longer. I was Jennie June. I approached him and said, 'What big, big strong hands you have! I bet you are a good fighter!' My aim was to talk babyishly so as gradually to betray my nature. 'If you and I had a fight, who do you think would win?'"

The young writer busted out laughing. "No!"

Jennie joined him in laughing. "I had no shame."

"What did the hulk say?"

Jennie twisted her face, and in a deep voice said, "'I could lick a dozen like yer together.' And then he tried to rob me."

"And you fought him off! Scratched and kicked him!"

"No," Jennie said warmly, as if in reverie. "I ran."

"Have you ever been down to Mulberry Street between Grand and Broome?"

"Yeah."

"What year were you born?"

"Nineteen-oh-six."

"Oh my. Well, if you had found yourself on Mulberry Street between Grand and Broome on an evening in November of 1892, you would have seen meandering slowly along from one side of the street to the other with a mincing gait, a haggard, tired-looking, short and slender youth between eighteen and nineteen, *moi*, clad in shabby clothes, and with a skullcap on my head. As I walk along, whenever I meet any robust, well-built young man of about my age, who is alone, I stop and address to him a few words. I roam through all the streets of the then dark and criminal Fourth Ward, occasionally halting near the groups of ruffians congregated in front of the barrooms . . .

"Finally, on the corner of Broome and Mulberry Streets, I address a tall, muscular, splendid specimen of the adolescent who, by the way, will later become a police officer. He continues in conversation with me, and I walk along by his side. I am soon seized with a sort of ague – due to sexual excitement – which causes my whole body to shake, and hardly permits me to speak . . . We finally pass out of sight down one of the dark covered alleys leading to tenements in the rear. His name was Red Mike."

Jennie stopped talking.

Red Mike, Red Mike.

She remembered him so vividly, the afterglow of their moment, their union. She thought she might cry.

"Go away, I want to be alone," she told the reporter. "Please. Please go away."

"Are you sure you're okay? I can help you to a cab."

"I don't need help from a –"

The young man disappeared.

An elegant old gentleman in a dark suit reached for her hand. He had a full head of white hair, cut close to his scalp.

"My name is Thomas, so happy to meet you," he said.

Lovers, continual lovers, only repay me.

"I met Walt in Gettysburg. He was my nurse."

Lovers, continual lovers.

A distorted voice blared from the speakers. "Welcome, ladies!"

Jennie awoke with a start, clutching herself. Am I okay? Am I alive?

Oh the memories, what they did to you in old age. Ghosts.

She remembered the old gentleman. What was his name? Thomas?

He was Walt Whitman's "adopted son." Whitman who turned forty and began his pursuit of adolescents.

When had she met the son?

It was 1896. Jennie had been a few years out of college, she'd been a boy named Earl Lind, shy, devout, easy to cry. Chatty, full of himself as Jennie June. He had moved to Manhattan in 1891 to go to college. An earnest, tiny boy, five feet five, 110 pounds. He had the wide hips, the narrow shoulders, his body safety-razored, chin hairs waxed.

In his spare time, he served as a missionary downtown, in the tenements. Full of virile temptation.

All the boys in high school had said he'd make a lovely girl.

Hello, pretty.

He came from a small town an hour outside the city. His family was upstanding merchant stock.

Within a few years of his arrival, even as "Earl" continued to work hard at school and to achieve respectable positions as an administrator, secretary, and editor, Jennie sliced a wide swath through every social class from the immigrant quarters to high society.

At the time she met Whitman's son, Jennie was working for the personal financial office of a millionaire, and, through acquaintances of the millionaire, she was invited to another millionaire's home for a fairy party in the suburbs north of the city.

Thomas, the "son," was nearly sixty by then. A veteran of the American War Between the States.

72

An acquaintance told Jennie of the Whitman connection before introducing them.

"My name is Thomas, so happy to meet you," he said.

"I'm Jennie June, and it is my pleasure."

An enormous mansion. Twelve bedrooms. Servants bustled through darkened staff doorways. A few dozen fairies stood in small groups, talking calmly and without a trace of the flamboyance that marked Jennie June's Bowery jaunts.

Jennie remembered that she had walked with Thomas to a quiet, lonely corner of the millionaire's parlor and lectured him on the androgynous qualities of Whitman's poetry – it was one of her less appealing personas, the college showoff.

"Whitman's work proves that he is the most prominent American fairy," Jennie had insisted. From memory, she quoted lines out of *Drum-Taps* and *Leaves of Grass*.

Of pure American breed, of reckless health, his body perfect.

"No wonder he became a nurse," Jennie went on. "Doesn't every fairy long to nurse a wounded, virile young man back to health? I believe that fairies can bring a fallen warrior back to his prime far faster than a female nurse."

There was a long silence. Thomas cleared his throat and gazed past Jennie.

"Do you disagree with my theory?"

73

And the elegant old man seemed to laugh at Jennie, and asked, "How do you think I met Walt, you little fool?"

Now, at the Faggots Ball, remembering those dismissive words, Jennie experienced a flush of regret and shame that surprised her. It was so long ago. So many years. Yet she couldn't forget her old dreams of turning a soldier into her lover.

Soldiers. They lived outside the city. Out near the edge of the frontier. But close enough for a Manhattan visitor.

They had been a last resort. Jennie had tried to love boys in the city. That hadn't worked out.

She had gone to Europe – heaven, but she couldn't stay there without a job.

She had gone west, out to the frontier. And that had been all the worse. The absolute worst.

She had gone in a caravan of fifty men of the roughest type: cowboys, miners, trappers, and thieves. All were bachelors or grass widowers. Day in and day out, they hardly talked of anything but prostitutes – fierce courtesans who enlivened every mining or lumbering camp of any permanence, charged seven times the rates in Manhattan, and salted away decent fortunes for their old age.

Jennie found the adolescent cowboys and miners of the Rockies the most prejudiced against effeminate males of any

74

of the hundreds of circles of young men with whom she had mingled as a girlboy.

Though Jennie was traveling as Earl, her male counterpart, it was not hard for the toughs to intuit her character. She feared an attack, or even murder. In the wilds of the Rockies, these men had easy opportunity to push her over a precipice.

Finally, though, after a dozen nights of sleeping in the same tent with these men, of listening to their bragging love stories, Jennie invited a cowboy for an evening's stroll in the forest. He had been brought up on a Wyoming ranch, never been inside a church, and could not read or write. He had once been a rough rider in Buffalo Bill's traveling show, and had performed in Madison Square Garden.

They talked about strong, self-confident men. Jennie got on a roll, painting a vivid picture of Davy Crockett.

Davy Crockett didn't bathe; he dressed in animal skins; he dropped out of school; he fought valiant, bloody battles with his friends, hired frontier whores, masturbated at every opportunity.

He lived among bears, with no civilizing culture to ensure an effeminate man's safety.

Oh, the way he subdued the wild animals, killed them all.

The way he subdued the Indian warriors, killed them all.

"I would love for such a virile man to subdue me," she said.

"What did you say?" the cowboy asked.

"I love you," Jennie said.

He knocked her to the ground.

Jennie explained that she was a woman trapped in a man's body against her will. She told him that she would love him the way no woman ever could.

He told her to be quiet if she wanted to live.

"Don't tell anyone! Please! Spare my life!" Jennie cried.

The cowboy stared at her long and hard, and then he promised to keep the incident their secret.

He left Jennie alone in the dark forest, and as slowly she regained her composure, she noticed the glinting eyes of bears in the surrounding trees.

She could hear them eating, just a hundred feet from her.

She could imagine them biting into her arms and legs, ripping her body apart.

She was terrified, but a familiar calmness overtook her fear.

What was it? What was she supposed to do?

Oh. Of course.

Prey.

She was used to being prey. As a practicing androgyne, she'd been chased by ferocious bears even in the bowels of Manhattan.

eir biceps: "I call you 'Strength'! I call you 'Power'! I call
man of iron! Mighty man of war! Mighty man of valor!
ty man of renown!"

er one who meets her for the first time asks: "Do you
ourself a girl? In all my life I never met a girl with
is!"

e found herself repeating the words out loud.
e had forgotten that she was alone at the Faggots Ball.
all my life I never met a girl with a penis!" she
d – before noticing that a small group of young drags
ettled a few steps from her. These youths appeared to
ofessional homosexuals. Not prostitutes, but that new
of leisurely men, the aesthetes and dilettantes who
ged their lives around parties, bars, and homosexual
rants.

ere Jennie had been lucky to designate one night
ek, at the most, to her sprees, these rouged drags
throw themselves into the scene nightly if it pleased

ey were sharing cocaine and laughing shrilly and gesturing
r direction.

exactly who they don't want to be, she said to herself.
their worst nightmare.

So she fell back on the survival techniques that had always
served her well.

Play dead, she told herself.

She made herself perfectly still.

Play dead.

She was wide awake all night, long after she heard the
bears scramble away.

Die, she told herself. Die.

Where the frontier had been a disaster, the barracks were
the most beguiling surprise.

She'd just turned twenty-six, and particularly on account of
her age, she had thought no more romantic adventures could
be hers. But it turned out that the next six years, even the last
of them, when she was thirty-one, were full of adventures as
romantic as any she had ever had.

When she dedicated herself to the career of a soldiers'
mignon, she was well aware that these men were particularly subject to venereal disease – and she ultimately
contracted anal and buccal venereal warts, syphilis, and
gonorrhea from them, whereas during her youth, from the
time she was sixteen until she turned twenty-five, she had
had close to seven hundred liaisons with civilian adolescents
without contracting any disease so far as she knew. But she

gladly assumed this greatly increased risk because of the ultravirility of soldiers.

How had she met the soldiers? In her usual manner, waltzing a familiar path through downtown Manhattan.

It was a sultry night. The man she fancied had a sheen of new perspiration soaking through his tight uniform.

"Oh, hello!" she said.

He was an artilleryman, and when they returned from the room he had rented for the evening, Jennie asked him if she might visit him at his barracks outside the city. She would worship him as she had in the room, she promised.

The next week, she made the journey. She was conducted to his squad room, but he was not in. She found herself in a sensual paradise containing about a dozen youthful soldiers busy at different things. She could not think of departing even though her friend was absent. She began to talk effeminately and babyishly. She was immediately hailed as a fairy, and shown to a seat on a bunk, having around her the arms of two soldiers, with several others sitting or lying on the same bunk and caressing her. It was almost the same as if a maiden had suddenly appeared in their midst. She outwomaned women for their entertainment.

She was so enthusiastically received t
little more than two years she visited th
one evening a week, devoting all the
scholarly pursuits in Manhattan.

For some weeks she enjoyed the rare
with her idols in a squad room or in
officer's private room, and had the run o
since practically everybody looked upon
unoffending tabby cat that might invac
was even put to bed in the barracks as
puts her babe in its cradle.

A typical evening in a squad roon
ing, the soldiers shout good-naturedly:
girl!"

"Hello, all you big braves!"

The rumor soon spreads to other squa
June" is making a visit, and a score o
about her. She always comes loaded o
and other things that soldiers are fond o
One youthful soldier after another rolls
displays tattooed figures for her to rav
you are completely masculine, and I w
it done." Others double back their right

of t
you
Mi

call
a p

blu
ha
be
cla
ar
re

a
co
th

in

I

78

79

So she fell back on the survival techniques that had always served her well.

Play dead, she told herself.

She made herself perfectly still.

Play dead.

She was wide awake all night, long after she heard the bears scramble away.

Die, she told herself. Die.

Where the frontier had been a disaster, the barracks were the most beguiling surprise.

She'd just turned twenty-six, and particularly on account of her age, she had thought no more romantic adventures could be hers. But it turned out that the next six years, even the last of them, when she was thirty-one, were full of adventures as romantic as any she had ever had.

When she dedicated herself to the career of a soldiers' mignon, she was well aware that these men were particularly subject to venereal disease – and she ultimately contracted anal and buccal venereal warts, syphilis, and gonorrhea from them, whereas during her youth, from the time she was sixteen until she turned twenty-five, she had had close to seven hundred liaisons with civilian adolescents without contracting any disease so far as she knew. But she gladly assumed this greatly increased risk because of the ultravirility of soldiers.

How had she met the soldiers? In her usual manner, waltzing a familiar path through downtown Manhattan.

It was a sultry night. The man she fancied had a sheen of new perspiration soaking through his tight uniform.

"Oh, hello!" she said.

He was an artilleryman, and when they returned from the room he had rented for the evening, Jennie asked him if she might visit him at his barracks outside the city. She would worship him as she had in the room, she promised.

The next week, she made the journey. She was conducted to his squad room, but he was not in. She found herself in a sensual paradise containing about a dozen youthful soldiers busy at different things. She could not think of departing even though her friend was absent. She began to talk effeminately and babyishly. She was immediately hailed as a fairy, and shown to a seat on a bunk, having around her the arms of two soldiers, with several others sitting or lying on the same bunk and caressing her. It was almost the same as if a maiden had suddenly appeared in their midst. She outwomaned women for their entertainment.

She was so enthusiastically received that for the period of a little more than two years she visited this military reservation one evening a week, devoting all the rest of her time to scholarly pursuits in Manhattan.

For some weeks she enjoyed the rare pleasure of associating with her idols in a squad room or in a noncommissioned officer's private room, and had the run of all the other rooms, since practically everybody looked upon her the same as on an unoffending tabby cat that might invade their quarters. She was even put to bed in the barracks as tenderly as a mother puts her babe in its cradle.

A typical evening in a squad room: On Jennie entering, the soldiers shout good-naturedly: "Hello, Jennie, old girl!"

"Hello, all you big braves!"

The rumor soon spreads to other squad rooms that "Jennie June" is making a visit, and a score or more soon gather about her. She always comes loaded down with cigarettes and other things that soldiers are fond of, except intoxicants. One youthful soldier after another rolls back his sleeve and displays tattooed figures for her to rave over: "That proves you are completely masculine, and I worship you for having it done." Others double back their right arms and let her feel of their biceps: "I call you 'Strength'! I call you 'Power'! I call you a man of iron! Mighty man of war! Mighty man of valor! Mighty man of renown!"

Later one who meets her for the first time asks: "Do you call yourself a girl? In all my life I never met a girl with a penis!"

She found herself repeating the words out loud.

She had forgotten that she was alone at the Faggots Ball.

"In all my life I never met a girl with a penis!" she blurted – before noticing that a small group of young drags had settled a few steps from her. These youths appeared to be professional homosexuals. Not prostitutes, but that new class of leisurely men, the aesthetes and dilettantes who arranged their lives around parties, bars, and homosexual restaurants.

Where Jennie had been lucky to designate one night a week, at the most, to her sprees, these rouged drags could throw themselves into the scene nightly if it pleased them.

They were sharing cocaine and laughing shrilly and gesturing in her direction.

I'm exactly who they don't want to be, she said to herself. I am their worst nightmare.

Jennie closed her eyes to blot out their existence, to return to her memories.

In the barracks, she was always outwardly modest. She frowned on decidedly improper advances, on the man who took her small hand in his large hand and placed it on his member, but lovemaking in private was another story.

She liked, for instance, to be regarded as the slave. In the "Enslaving Ceremony," she lay prostrate on the floor; her companion towered above her, placed his foot on her head, and pronounced her his slave. She had always felt that a woman should adore her husband so much as to delight in being treated as a slave, and to suffer gladly any abuse by her lord.

In the "Ceremony of Adoration," her companion stood upright, she prostrated herself, clasped his legs, pressed her lips against his feet, recited all the heroic qualities which enslaved her to him, and cried out over and over again her love and adoration for him. The soldiers said they only hoped they would ultimately secure a wife who would adore them as Jennie did.

But her degradation, and the pleasure that some infantrymen took in it, soon set a minority against her.

She became a laughingstock.

And her troops had their orders. They were shipping off –
to Texas, to Indianapolis.

One soldier found her on the Bowery and told her,
"We've been talking about ya. We thought, we thought
you might . . ."

She was called upon to say goodbye – as she feared, forever
– to her much-coveted position of pet of the fort.

The day of their departure, she could not go to work. She
was too nervous, too sad.

At the hour, she met them at the station. A dozen were
in the train windows, a dozen of them chanting, all as one,
"Three cheers for Jennie June!"

She waved to them from the tracks. She held her favorite
silk scarf.

She tried to sing one of her songs before the train had gone
– disappearing into the sunset.

She had a fine treble voice and she stamped down her foot
and sang a line from memory, "The night I first met my fierce
Murphy!"

She heard applause.

"Excuse me, my name is Gabriel, and I wonder if you know
that you are singing?"

Jennie tried to focus on the fairy standing in front of her. Slight, simpering, dark hair.

Several of the fairy's friends had gathered around Jennie – they had taken her by the arms, they were walking her, leading her toward the bandstand.

"We have a volunteer!" shouted the MC, who appeared to be dolled up as a red monkey in a hoop skirt.

"The lights are so bright," Jennie whispered.

The fairies were lifting her onto the catwalk.

"Oh, for a star, for a star like you. With your pretty voice. The crowd demands it!"

"Ladies and ladies and gentlemen," shouted the MC.

A little man ran from the bandstand and asked her the song.

"To the tune of 'My Bonnie Lies Over the Ocean,'" she said.

The little man returned to the band.

"Ladies and gentlemen," shouted the MC. "We are proud to give you . . ."

"Jennie June," Jennie stage-whispered.

"Ladies and gentlemen," shouted the MC. "We are proud to give you the beautiful Jennie June."

She stood in the spotlight, immobilized by the memory of what had really happened when she returned to the barracks to wish them farewell.

She had not sung one of her songs.

She had not been invited to share a goodbye with her braves.

A corporal had attacked her, punching her face until Jennie's fingers, cupped over her eyes to protect them, were dripping blood that ran down her forearms.

"Please, please," she screamed, "let this be enough! Don't ya see you've already knocked one of my eyes out of its socket?"

The corporal allowed her to escape, and she made her way back to the city, to the hospital, where a doctor wrote a full description of her injuries to accompany charges, should she wish to place them.

She took her complaint to the U.S. district attorney's office, but as soon as she had finished telling him what had happened, the man simply dismissed her.

Next she went to the police, but since she'd been attacked on a military reservation, the police and civil courts had no powers, no jurisdiction.

Finally, because the assault had made its way into the paper, a military secretary at Governor's Island, in New York Harbor, put a colonel in charge of a military hearing.

It lasted about three hours, and Jennie was questioned as if she were the one under charges. At the close of the hearing, there was a motion to dismiss, and the official reason announced to the room was that Jennie, addicted to sex, had indecently accosted her assailants.

"This is a song I wrote," she said. Her legs were shaking. "I wrote it for a soldier I loved. The song is 'My Fierce Murphy.'"

The band kick-started the melody. The audience hushed.

Jennie planted her feet and lurched her chest forward and put her chin up, eyes squeezed shut, and sang at the top of her voice:

> The night I first met my fierce Murphy,
> He punched me and kicked me and stoned;
> He sent me away all in tatters,
> I screamed and I wept and I moaned.
> But I loved him, I loved him,
> I loved him more than I can tell, can tell!
> I loved him, I loved him,
> I loved him more than I can tell!

She felt a surge of power rise up her legs into her chest and she sang higher, louder.

> He was the next time even fiercer,
> He snatched me up, threw me outside;

But while I was held in his clutches,
My face in his blouse I did hide.
I loved him, I loved him,
That moment I was in his arms, strong arms!
I loved him, I loved him,
That moment I was in his arms!

There were whistles. A woman shouted, "Yes, yes, yes, you were in his arms!"

The third time he said he'd me marry,
This wonderful, wonderful brave!
I then was so robbed of my reason,
I nothing did but for him rave.
I loved him, I loved him,
I nothing did but for him rave – yes, rave!
I loved him, I loved him,
I nothing did but for him rave!

She summoned every bit of power she had in her, and then fell into a tense, softly whispered baritone, the male voice she'd never accepted.

I'm dying, I'm dying, I'm dying,
For love of this wonderful brave;
I'm dying, I'm dying, I'm dying –
Will he not show mercy and save?
Dying – dying –
I see yawn for me the dark grave, dread grave!
Dying – dying –
Will he not show mercy and save?

At the exact moment that she concluded her song, Jennie threw open her eyes to take in the audience. She saw the judges, deep in conversation yet watching her from the corner of their eyes. Up in the VIP boxes, she saw Talullah Bankhead or a drag who looked just like the actress. She saw Blanche Dunn, who couldn't bother with a smile. And then, with a gasp, she saw A'Lelia Walker, eyes locked on hers.

"It's not safe here!" Jennie shouted.

The sound of the crowd welled up, drowning Jennie's voice, and the band conspired to drive her from the stage. A bottle landed at her feet and shattered. She was bleeding. Her eye swelled shut. It throbbed, the pain shooting back through her temples.

Her ears rang.

She looked up, trying to see with one eye.

She couldn't find A'Lelia.

CHAPTER SIX

Nancy Cunard, the steamship heiress, fixed her polar blues on Langston Hughes as he passed her in the aisle behind the box seats in the upper tier of the Manhattan Casino.

"Langston! Are you ignoring me?" She twisted her face and laughed to herself, as if it were impossible that he might do just that. She wore a slip of a dress, with the frailest straps holding the front to the back. Her long white arms were covered from wrist to shoulder with bracelets. African ivory.

"Nancy," he murmured. "Nancy."

"Langston!" She tossed her short pale hair and briskly pushed herself closer to him. She picked at his lapel, smiling. "I've got to tell you, Salvador Dalí is dying to meet you! I've been on him for quite some time, you know, to explore Harlem. I think that his work will fall behind, you see, if he continues to ignore this new idiom of the American Negro. Don't you quite agree?"

By ever so slightly pulling his shoulders back, Langston was able to reclaim some of the space that separated him from

Nancy, but before he could answer her she had thrown her arms up to call out his name again – "Langston!" – and caught him across the tip of his chin with the thick band of ivory that clenched her elbow.

He fell back a step. "That will be enough of that, Nancy," he said, rubbing his face. He took another step backward and asked if Henry, her jazz player boyfriend, was with her.

"Henry is not particularly comfortable with this world. There is only so much Carl Van Vechten I can endure, for instance. He is a fraud, Langston. Why do you defend him? You do. You defend him. I know that if I continue to criticize his shit novels, his horrid exploitative tripe, his sublimated lust for every black man who is unfortunate enough to be 'immortalized' in his novels, whatever I say, you will defend him, and I don't understand that."

"Well, Nancy, for one thing, Carl and I have a good back and forth. I mean, he listens very carefully – "

She interrupted. "Have I told you of the piece I'm writing? For *The Crisis*? I'm calling it 'Does Anyone Know Any Negroes?' After a conversation I had with my mother. That was the question she asked me, after I told her about Henry. And she was so, just, just, puzzled. She looked at me, in a daze, and said, 'You mean to say they go into people's houses?'"[10]

Langston was looking past Nancy, transfixed by the spectacle, down on the dance hall runway, of the loose-skinned, bony drag who, in a deep booming voice, was singing,

> I'm dying, I'm dying, I'm dying,
> For love of this wonderful brave;
> I'm dying, I'm dying, I'm dying –
> Will he not show mercy and save?
> Dying – dying –
> I see yawn for me the dark grave, dread grave!
> Dying – dying –
> Will he not show mercy and save?

"Langston!" Nancy shouted, taking him by the shoulder. "Where are you? Oh, who is that ofay bitch you're watching? What is she up to? Oh, it's awful, it's pathetic. Langston, don't you think I have a duty to expose my mother's racism?"

"What?" Langston smiled sweetly. "What did you say, Nancy?"

CHAPTER SEVEN

The rouge, the deadly eyes, the sparkling gown. The high, high squealing voice warning A'Lelia that she was in danger.

She tried to break her gaze from the old drag's, she tried to close her eyes – and then, as she finally managed to turn away, to force herself to look at the faces in the upper tier, in the box seats, a stoic, heavy-lidded face came to the front of a black-tie crowd and stared at Lelia with deadly intent.

She knew him. She knew that man. One of Dutch Schultz's men – Bo, his name was Bo, Bo Weinberg.

"It's true!" she shouted. "Mayme, find that police officer!"

"What's wrong? What's wrong?"

"Just find him, Mayme. Tell him I'll pay him."

"I'll go," Mayme said, "but you sit down. You sit down."

A'Lelia lost her footing and fell backward to the floor.

Everything went dark.

"Where's Mayme?" she gasped. "Mayme? I can't see anything."

*   *   *

Her mother flashed into her mind's eye in the elaborate dress of an Egyptian queen. Her headpiece glittered. The skin around her eyes was tattooed. Her throat was choked with platinum and diamond necklaces in the shape of adders.

A'Lelia had skimmed Freud. She had had her dreams explicated, in painstaking detail, by a woman she'd met in Paris who promised, in a flawless growl, to "frighten" the bad spirits away from Lelia if only she would burn an orange candle at her bedside every night for a week, ending on the night of the blood moon.

She knew that this vision of her mother was a warning from a deep recess of her subconscious, but still she wondered, as she lay there on the floor of the VIP box at the Manhattan Casino, why Madame had to come cloaked with all the trappings of antiquity to scare the life out of her daughter?

Are you that disappointed, Mother? A'Lelia asked.

Madame's arms rose slowly. Her golden breastplate shimmered.

Mother? A'Lelia asked. Have I? Have I done everything wrong?

Yes, baby, Madame murmured. Everything.

An attendant passed a gold tray in front of Madame, who without taking her eyes from her daughter's removed the plain white envelope, postmarked 1918, from the shiny surface.

Slowly, she removed a folded sheet of translucent paper from it, unfolded it, said, Oh, A'Lelia, it's for you.

No! A'Lelia shouted. Don't. Please don't.

She knew that it was one of the begging letters, from some poor soul who had seen her picture in the papers.

Let's just see what it says. Madame began to read.

Dear Mrs. Walker,

I saw the pictures of your trip to Paris, France. It made me feel so glad, seeing you walk so proud. The clothes you wore were so pretty, I fell asleep thinking about them. I woke up and my fingers were rubbing together like I was touching the silks and minks, testing them to see if they were good enough for me, just the way I imagine you do when you walk into the stores over there in Europe.

I would love for just one day to walk into my house dressed in one of your dresses, with soft silk hose and high heels. I do think it would be something else to walk into my house and say I AM TELLING YOU TO WATCH OUT I AM LEAVING YOU!

Oh Mrs. Walker he didn't ever love me. Beats me with my hair brush. Throws me onto the bed and rips my skirt up the whole way to my back and beats me with the bristles until I am bleeding and crying.

We live with his cousins and they don't do nothing to stop it because they tell me it is my fault. I'm stupid. Lazy. It's cause of me we have no money. Cause of me going to the hospital.

I will light this house on fire, Mrs. Walker. I will kill him and kill the rest of them, too.

Or I won't. Or I will just be here for the rest of my life.

Madame paused. She slowly removed her headpiece and moved to place it on her daughter's head.

By the time A'Lelia reached her decadent prime, spending cash the way only the second-generation rich can spend cash, her mother had already passed into legend.

Madame C. J. Walker was born Sarah Breedlove in rural Louisiana, in a weathered shack, five years after Abraham Lincoln signed the Emancipation Proclamation. She got married at fourteen because she wanted a house of her own, she said, and at seventeen she gave birth to Lelia, her only child. The year was 1885.

The South into which Lelia was born was a militarized, sickly society. Many southerners hoped to overthrow the occupying soldier reconstructionists. The KKK terrorized the emancipated; the nurses let the frail die; local businesses proceeded as if nothing in the world would please them more than to hire black people at some point in the future, when they were forced to at gunpoint. Nothing dissuaded crusaders in the press and pulpit from finding new words to mislabel the habits that slavery, poverty, and humiliation had, with brute force, woven into black family life.

With freedom came greater mobility, which the national press, especially the tabloids, found alarming. In the popular New York press, newspapers such as the lurid *National Police Gazette*, the fate of black Americans, post–Civil War, was covered with racist "humor" and queasy sexual speculation. In one cautionary story about the light-skinned Lowre Gang of North Carolina, southern criminals who'd lie in wait for U.S. cavalry, the *Gazette* emphasized the evil of its darkest-skinned member, a black woman:

It is supposed that the Lowres themselves are tainted with the blood of Ethiopia, and it is but natural, therefore, for them to affiliate with blacks, many of whom they press into their service, but too willingly, betraying their employers and bringing ruin upon the men and women who have hitherto been their best friends. Prominent among these sneaks . . . is a big overgrown wench known to the band as "Big Black Kate," who for low and contemptible cunning shrewdness is noted among them above all others. She is a greasy fat monster, with a yellow eye in her black head . . . Her entire happiness consists in cohabiting with these rascals – on the Victoria Woodhull free-love principle – in drinking bad rum and carousing, and in prying about the country picking up facts for the infamous gang she thoroughly and faithfully serves.[11]

And in one "humorous" account of a midwestern lynching, the *Gazette* wrote that "rather than pay a Negro waiter a fee of twenty-five cents on a steamer at Dubuque, Iowa, last week, a passenger shot him. A warning to extortionate waiters."

The tabloids pointed to Italians as murderers, Chinese as opium pushers, Irish as bullying brawlers, and Jews as monopolists and thieves. Every color and creed who settled a new block of big, thriving northern cities was ripe for ridicule in the penny press. But only blacks could be murdered rather than paid.

And it was hardly the penny press alone that published racist tracts. Even "enlightened" and celebrated brotherhood-of-man types used racist ammunition to argue against slavery.

In an 1857 editorial in the Brooklyn *Daily Times*, democratic, free-loving, song-of-himself singer Walt Whitman wrote that blacks were in their own country degraded, cruel, almost bestial, the victims of cruel chiefs, and of bloody religious rites – their lives never secure – no education, no refinement, no elevation, no political knowledge – such is the general condition of the African tribes. From these things they are sold to the American plantations.

Would we then defend the slave-trade? No; we would merely remind the reader that, in a large view of the case, the change is not one for the worse, to the victims of that trade. The blacks, mulattoes, etc., either in the Northern or Southern States, might bear in mind that had their forefathers remained in Africa, and their birth occurred there, they would now be roaming Krumen or Ashanteemen, wild, filthy, paganistic – not residents of a land of light, and bearing their share, to some extent, in all its civilizations.

It is also to be remembered that no race ever can remain slaves if they have it in them to become free. Why do the slave ships go to Africa only?

The worst results of the slave trade are those mainly caused by attempts of the government to outlaw it. We speak of the horrors of the "middle passage," – the wretched, suffocating, steaming, thirsty, dying crowds of black men, women and children, packed between decks in cutter-built ships, modelled not for space, but speed. This, we repeat, is not an inherent attribute of the slave trade, but of declaring it piracy.[12]

Lelia's father, Moses McWilliams, died before she turned six. As the Walker women's fame grew, legend spread that Moses had died in a brutal lynching after an 1888 riot, but neither Madame Walker nor A'Lelia ever confirmed that McWilliams was murdered.

Madame Walker's early drive to create a home for herself grew a thousand times over following A'Lelia's birth, but she knew that hard work alone wasn't going to undo the disadvantages she faced as the free-born daughter of slaves, a single mother in a racist society.

Following her husband's death in 1889, Madame and three-year-old Lelia moved to St. Louis, part of the vast migration of rural southern blacks to the country's industrial cities. No home waited for her, no job. It was, as her great-great-granddaughter, A'Lelia Bundles, wrote in her definitive biography of the Walkers, a plain case of "raw determination" that propelled Madame Walker.

St. Louis, like Philadelphia, New York, Washington, D.C., and Indianapolis, was a city divided and subdivided a dozen times over along class, race, and money lines. One prominent black St. Louis resident, Cyprian Clamorgan, had, thirty years before the Walkers' arrival, published the pamphlet *The Colored Aristocracy of St. Louis,* with the stated purpose of showing "the origins and position of a portion of those whom circumstances have placed in the path of comparative respectability and to whom fortune has been kind in the bestowal of the good gifts of life."

Clamorgan, of Haitian, Welsh, Portuguese, and African descent, illustrated the class structure in St. Louis by example of his own family, the property they owned, their education and influence. It was his father, Jacques, who, arriving in St. Louis from Haiti, found work as a fur trader, entrepreneur, and explorer, claiming thousands of acres of land across Missouri and Kansas. He was an opportunist who falsely claimed to have Spanish land grants to the property he seized. He was a slave owner. But the second generation, as represented by Jacques's son, Cyprian, lived in the manner of European elites, obsessed with education, manners, home decor, clothing, hairstyles, and high culture.

These elites were rich, and for the most part they were very fair skinned, "separated from the white race by a line of division so faint that it can be traced only by the keen eye of prejudice."[13]

The elite counted among its professionals doctors, lawyers,

judges, entrepreneurs, and barbers, who were known as "tonsorial artists."

Poor people, then as now, were blamed by the country's elite for their degraded circumstances. They lived in slums because they didn't value privacy, because they didn't know how to work hard or were lazy or genetically predisposed to beastly behavior. The bell curve of history had "proved" their inferiority to the ruling rich classes.

One historian, Philip Bruce, published a critically acclaimed bestseller, *The Plantation Negro As a Freeman*, in 1889 that blamed the poverty of the black family on defects in its parents, who let their boys roam too freely and encouraged their girls' promiscuity.

The black elites frequently took the same opinions, mimicking the diversions and prejudices of the white upper class, with whatever translations were necessary to remove themselves from the low labels.

In St. Louis, despite the comparative freedom from terroristic racial politics, Madame Walker, uneducated, could find only menial work.

Her instinct was to diversify her labor, to use her seemingly limitless energy in search of a way up from poverty. She worked as a "sudbuster," or washerwoman; she went to night school; she was a volunteer at her church and charities in her adopted St. Louis – fighting the snobbery of the light-skinned, established black society of the 1890s. She knew that it would take the work and wits of a half-dozen women to lift her beloved daughter, A'Lelia, from their downtown St. Louis neighborhood of hookers, bathhouses, and bare-knuckle dive bars.

Overwork, motherhood, and the complications of a troubled new marriage nearly overwhelmed Madame Walker, but it was the outward, ugly manifestation of her anguish – an affliction of the scalp – that finally showed her the escape route from drudgery.

The scabs, the swelling, the itch that won't go away – profound dandruff and psoriasis is a plague that undermines a person's sense of self-control. The body is overproducing skin, almost as if in allergic reaction. Swelling, flakes, sores, scabs – the body is overreacting for all the world to see. In Madame Walker's case, her locks were breaking off in her hands, leaving the sides of her head stubbled and sore. She felt hideous, as if her appearance reflected a kind of psychic flaw. At that rock-bottom moment when the basic human instinct for wound licking, for retreat, usually wins out, Madame Walker took to her bed and had a dream, a deep-sleep vision that changed her life.

She dreamed of a "big black man" who told her precisely which ingredients to mix to save her scalp: beeswax, petrolatum, coconut oil, copper sulfate, precipitated sulfur, the scent of lavender. Following her own laboratory experiments, Walker settled on a formula; soon her hair and scalp problems were history, and in a few years her products and salons were spreading across the country.

In 1910, Madame Walker moved the company to Indianapolis, and the company would reach the pinnacle of its success there. Indiana had a thriving black professional and business class, and was one of the country's biggest manufacturing cities.

Perhaps coincidentally, in the nineteenth century, Indiana had been associated with liberal divorce laws which freed some women from tortured marriages. Even in 1864, the *National Police Gazette* had complained that

> by the aid of a set of unscrupulous lawyers in this city [people] can get divorced as often as they please. It is no longer necessary, in giving full license to their lusts, to expose themselves to the annoyance of being brought into court . . . The libertine, male or female, is thus able to contract as many marriages and procure as many divorces as he or she likes, the only limit being the time required to rush the formalities through the Courts. These Courts,

it is hardly necessary to mention, are the State Courts of Indiana. Where else would such an outrage in the form of law be tolerated?[14]

In Indianapolis, black society was divided by skin color, but Madame Walker had already begun to break free of the rules that applied to less accomplished women. Free from men who didn't respect her, she lived autonomously. As her company revenues increased, she simply contacted people she thought of as peers, introduced herself, and made connections.

If you look through the black newspapers of the early twentieth century, you'll see that Madame Walker was not the first entrepreneur to create a formula to care for black women's hair. Straighteners, bleaches, balms, ointments – subtle variations, lawsuits over formula poaching, fights for the top-producing sales agents. But none of her rivals possessed Madame Walker's cool instinct for the jugular: like the industrial titans of the Gilded Age, Madame Walker thrived by outmarketing and outsmarting the competition, by making brilliant distribution alliances, by choking suppliers who tried to gain an inch on her, by understanding her customer down to the heartbeat. The historian James Weldon Johnson notes in his landmark 1930 book *Black Manhattan* that Walker "taught the masses of coloured women . . . the secret of the enhancement of female beauty, and on it she built a business that covered not only the United States but the West Indies. She . . .made a fortune and died in her own luxurious home . . ."

But her business was only one part of her legacy; Madame Walker also made her transformative mark through her philanthropy and political activism.

This "big brown woman the color of parched peanuts," before whom "all Harlem and the black Eastern Seaboard bourgeois began ducking and bowing,"[15] donated record-breaking sums to the NAACP and to black branches of the YMCA. She chaired the executive committee of the Colored Women's Motor Corps, which carried wounded soldiers upon their return to the States from World War I; lobbied the U.S. Senate for action on racial inequalities; used an array of business alliances to bring black economic clout to bear in the fight against lynching; and, as her business grew, began to reorganize it as "an enterprise on a grand scale controlled by black women with political and civic objectives."[16]

A'Lelia had tried so hard to be like her mother. When she was younger it had seemed as if she might have succeeded.

A'Lelia was the one who, in 1913, had insisted that Madame open the luxurious salon in Harlem; A'Lelia had traveled to the Caribbean and South America to preach the Walker creed and discern the cultural differences that might complicate their expansion plans; A'Lelia joined the U.S. Navy League, the civilian group, founded in 1902 at Teddy Roosevelt's urging, that educated the country on naval activities.

Like Madame Walker, A'Lelia was an adult before she acquired, with all haste, a sweet tooth for high living. Clothing and jewels and gilded furniture and extravagant parties.

The trappings helped draw attention to Madame's political and social agenda. No careworn scrubwoman, however eloquent, could get the press to pay attention to her opinions on military segregation and the need to put teeth into the antilynching laws that were on the books.

A'Lelia used her access to life's luxuries to serve her causes, too, but her philanthropies came early in her life, with none of Madame's philosophical pragmatism.

A'Lelia threw a Fourth of July celebration for the president of Liberia. She donated money to the Tuskegee Institute and the NAACP. But nothing felt as good as the hands-on good works she'd performed as a youth.

As a young woman, she had kept three cars; she loved to drive long distances, to zoom down empty country roads. So when the war effort needed her, she was a natural captain of the motor corps of the Circle for Negro War Relief during

World War I, when she drove wounded soldiers in an ambulance to the veterans' hospitals upon their return from the theater of war.

Driving the ambulance, she would listen to the soldiers talk; they talked as if they had just regained their voices. Their lives had cracked open, and it seemed that they had to keep talking just so they didn't lose everything that had been dear to them – their wives and girlfriends and baby daughters, their buddies who stayed on, still healthy, fighting, their lost buddies.

They always remembered the way their buddies had died, and it seemed they wanted to sear the images on Lelia's soul: the burst of bullets, the wall of men pouring toward them, the buzz of a distant battle, growing louder and louder.

They would tell her she was pretty. They would ask for a kiss or just a smile.

They would tell her she had the prettiest hair.

"Turn around and smile at me. I want to see something nice."

It always seemed to be a sunny morning, the days she drove. A soft sky, the *mmmmmm* of the tires on the road.

She saw in some of these soldiers that thing she had loved so much in John Robinson, her first husband, the only one she'd loved the way she thought a woman should love a man.

She had loved his quiet confidence when she met him as a

wide-smiling fifteen-year-old, in Pittsburgh at the Fort Smith Hotel, where he was a telephone operator.

She had loved his dark brown skin and the shape of him – not too tall, but with a good strong physique.

She was meant to be coupled. She knew that from an early age, just as she knew that if she was going to be happy she had to make her own place in the world, out from under her mother's landscape-altering wingspan.

The trick was in making it all work.

CHAPTER EIGHT

Harold Jackman, the British lovely, the swaggering man-about-town, everybody's favorite loverboy, male model, rumor-making playboy, subject of Richmond Barthe's luscious art, had no fucking idea how he'd ended up broken away from his too-too-hot set, Caska Bonds, the voice coach; Blanche Dunn, the existential goddess; and those gorgeous Italians who'd kept gripping his thigh.

He had gone for a walk. He had wanted to clear his head.

He had caught the end of the wretched song and dance and, well, he had to admit he had thought it would make a good story to tell, a letter to write to his boy Countee, Countee Cullen, his best man in the world and a famous poet to boot.

So he had gone to the edge of the stage and offered his hand, offered his good-looking hand to the creature who'd just completed her terrible musical number.

"May I escort you through the crowd?" he had asked her.

"Harold!" Blanche had shouted from her box. "Harold, you're so gallant!"

Caska had sidled up next to him and kissed his ear. "This has got to be photographed. You hold on to this monster until I find a drunk photographer. I cannot believe you, Harold."

"A small lady always appreciates a strong young man's help; I do thank you," said Jennie June, taking his hand and stepping down from the runway where she'd just performed.

Jackman paused to nod. He was surprised to find he had a lump in his throat. Something about the tiny voice. The old girl – she had such a tiny, kind voice.

"That was brave," Jackman said.

"Oh, I'm not brave," Jennie demurred. "And I'm not much of an entertainer, compared to these new girls."

Jackman chuckled before he could stop himself, and then, just as quickly, apologized. "That was a rude laugh, or so they tell me every couple of days."

"Oh, I'm used to rudeness. Now let's find a dark quiet corner where we can get to know one another."

Jackman stopped in his tracks and looked up at Blanche's box. "Help!" he mouthed silently, but continued in the direction Jennie led him.

Jackman had found himself depleted this morning when he woke, depleted all day at school, teaching boys whose voices and posture were so *young* that it made him feel embarrassed for himself, where life had taken him, how he had suddenly gotten old, twenty-seven. He had old man ailments, the stomach problems, headaches, and an emptiness of heart that hadn't originated in a tragic loss. Or had it?

Jackman, standing here at the Faggots Ball with scrawny pale Jennie June, found himself thinking of Kate, a friend of friends – Kate, with her exaggerated, off-pitch ladylikeness, was this comic figure, and Jackman was prone to laughter. At her expense. He told himself that Kate couldn't tell he thought her ridiculous, but the truth was he could see the hurt in her eyes every time he saw her.

He was a vicious mimic, he was an unforgivable gossip.

He knew that Langston in particular had grounds to call him a cruel prick, the way Jackman poked fun at his uneducated mother.

But he'd see Langston dragging his mother to Harlem parties – the mother tipping-over drunk, with her bad English and her funny, naïve presumptions to elegance, and it made him fucking laugh.

He knew what it was that made him look mirthfully for a weak spot and then poke at it and poke at it and poke at it. Or rather he knew where it had started. With Countee. In high school. Being black in an all-white school, they had shrouded themselves with a nasty wit, a private wit. They had met at DeWitt Clinton, at Fifty-ninth Street and Tenth Avenue. George Cukor and Fats Waller had been a few years ahead of them; Lionel Trilling, just a year.

Jackman used to nag Cullen about being, well, blacker, being from the South, Louisville: "Oh those must be *your* people," he'd say, whenever someone black did something dumb, misused or made up a word.

Countee would double back on him with something equally bad.

· He liked to think it was just leftover adolescent foolishness, what was left between Countee and him. There was no one else who was on his exact wavelength. No one else would laugh at his elaborate absurd little stories: Bessie White "passing" for white, but being done in by her weakness for ham bologna.

Well, except maybe Langston, but Langston was too hard to be with. Too busy being innocent.

Was it just that despite the parties, the lovers, his lovely, amazing daughter, the fame he had achieved among the intimidating, scholarly artists and writers who were his friends, he was missing his best friend Countee, and wanted him to come home?

Jackman knew that the chattering class of Harlem had split

open with laughter when he traveled to Europe with Countee for the big honeymoon voyage, after Countee married W. E. B. DuBois's rotten daughter, Yolanda. The headlines were jokes, a hundred variations on "Groom Sets Sail with Best Man, Bride Stays Home."

But Countee had wanted so badly to get married, to marry into royalty. He had wanted to be in a family so badly. Adopted by the Very Reverend Frederick Cullen, the influential pastor of Harlem's most influential Episcopal church, taken into the inner circle of W. E. B. DuBois, who championed his highly formal poetry in *The Crisis*, the trouble with Countee was he was just born to be respectable.

So, the marriages.

So, the obsession with his place in the pantheon.

So, the alliances and feuds with every powerful black man who held a position in the literary world.

But for Jackman, the true Countee was the boy who'd scrawled, beneath a photo of himself and Jackman on the beach in their swimsuits, the words *Damon and Pythias*. Mythological friends, Damon and Pythias were undyingly faithful, like a married couple. When Dionysius condemned one to death, the other stood in his place so the condemned could tend to his final affairs. At the hour of execution, the condemned returned to take his companion's place – he would never have let his friend die for him, though his friend would have done so.

Dionysius was so surprised by the depth of their friendship that he spared the condemned's life, and let them both live.

They found themselves seated on the bottom stairs at the rear of the hall, away from the noise. Jackman nursed what was left in his flask.

"You have the wrong idea," he said. "I'm not trying to seduce you."

Now it was Jennie's turn to chuckle. "Of course not. You, you are far too handsome. I am your grandmother's age, I'm sure. Women must melt before you. I'm not wrong, am I. You are quite the sport, my man."

"I've been called a shiek, but never a sport."

"Ah, but the shieks are slightly effeminate, aren't they. The lady's men. Valentino himself was effeminate, wasn't he? And these men who model themselves after him, these *shieks*, they are, on the spectrum of masculinity, closer to an androgyne like me than to an absolute *man* like you. I bet you have never been with a man."

Jackman didn't answer.

"You are indeed a sport!" Jennie said. "I see it in the way you swagger."

"The sporting life," Jackman chuckled. "You mean the games people play? Gamblers? Boxers?"

"And carousers! And the virile. The promiscuous men, out on the town, sowing their seed with every woman they meet. And when there are no women available, then a fairy would do." Jennie settled into her seat on the cold stairs. Despite everything, she had started to get more comfortable.

By the time Jennie June hit the city in the 1890s, the "sport" tag she was trying to affix to Jackman was a common label for the growing class of young, urban bachelors who'd rather be out all night, at the boxing match, the cockfight, and the high-stakes poker game; in a prostitute's bed, silk sheets of the most elegant brothel, or a soiled cot in the smoky back room of a dive.

Sports came from rich and poor families, though it was the rising middle class, the office workers, clerks, administrators, who saw this commitment to sexual abandon, reckless games, and after-hours carousing as a way to keep that feminine trap, the family, the nice home, at bay.

Sports cultivated a lifestyle that inspired the newly rising pop-trash press to cover murder, prostitution, and blood sports with detailed, salacious intensity. The murder in 1836 of the prostitute Helen Jewett set off a battle for circulation among newspapers that, learning on the job, put the trial of Jewett's sport lover on the front pages for a year.

The "sporting" press, the *Whip,* the *Sporting Whip,* and the *Rake* among them, championed promiscuity, mistresses, and prostitutes. There were more bachelors in town. Men who had moved to town on their own were waiting longer to find Wife #1. And men who had gotten themselves married already found it easy to join their single friends in upscale saloons and brothels.

Young boys, twelve-year-olds running with their older, wiser brothers, found themselves a favorite brothel. In the 1850s, Walt Whitman used a piece in the Brooklyn *Daily Times* to address this shift in the culture:

After dark, in the great City of New York, any man passing along Broadway, between Houston and Fulton Streets, finds the western sidewalk full of prostitutes, jaunting up and down there, by ones, twos, or threes – on the look-out for customers. Many of these girls are quite handsome, have a good-hearted appearance and, in encouraging circumstances, might make respectable and happy women.

Some of these prostitutes have their own rooms, and "keep house" by themselves; others live in the usual establishments on a larger scale, owned by some old or middle-aged women, and tenanted by six, eight or a dozen prostitutes. Of late, there are a great many cellars – dancing places, a number of them German – where the principal business is prostitution. There are not a few in Canal Street, and in Greenwich Street; and indeed they are to be found in all parts of the city.

The hardest houses of all are those in Cherry, Water, and Walnut Streets, and around the Five Points. Here the prostitutes are generally drunkards. Sailors, canal-boatmen, young fellows from the country . . . go regularly there. You see the women half exposed at the cellar doors as you pass. Their faces are flushed and pimpled. The great doings in these quarters are at night. Then, besides the prostitution, there are dances, rum drinking, fights, quarrels, and so on.

Though of course not acknowledged or talked about, or even alluded to, in "respectable society," the plain truth is that nineteen out of twenty of the mass of American young men, who live in or visit the great cities, are more or less familiar with houses of prostitution and are customers to them . . .

Especially of the best classes of men under forty years of age, living in New York and Brooklyn, the mechanics, apprentices, sea-faring men, drivers of horses, butchers, machinists, the custom is to go among prostitutes as an ordinary thing. Nothing is thought of it – or rather the wonder is, how can there be any "fun" without it . . .

Why is marriage getting less and less in repute – a weaker and weaker tie? And why is the sneaking and filthy practice of men of means supporting kept women for themselves becoming more and more common?

. . . Why not a candid and courageous course pursued by writers and speakers upon the subject of sexuality? How shall we escape coming to that at last?

Is not every young man, every girl – every person of any age – desirous of having a powerful, agreeable, clear-fleshed, sweet-blooded body? And through this universal wish, could not human pollution in all its forms be best attacked, and put down?[17]

"There were different strata of sport," Jennie said.

"White and black?" Jackman teased. "Christian and Jew? Italian and Greek?"

"Well, that isn't what I – " Jennie stammered. "You are, well, less likely to hear an exposition on Harlem from me than from your darling Carl Van Vechten."

"I'm jesting," Jackman said. "You didn't pay attention to

black people in 1895, did you? Didn't think so. I know I can't trust what you'd say about black people in 1850. Hell – you're not that old! Hell, you're a young gal, now that I got you talking about the old days. You've got color in the cheeks."

"But, actually, I can tell you about one black fairy, from the 1830s. Her name was Mary Jones."

"Mary Jones! That's a delicate name!" Jackman pursed a wry smile. "Mary Jones indeed. Tell me about Mary Jones."

"Mary Jones lived in a brothel on Greene Street. He'd clean and cook, that sort of thing," Jennie said.

"Of course."

"He loved the way that he looked in women's clothes. I don't think you understand that, do you? You don't enjoy an elegant, delicate dress, the way the silk hangs on your leg and you see the play of fabric in the mirror."

Jackman smiled and shook his head. No.

"Well, Mary Jones did. And it was enough to get her put in jail. They didn't care if men went to extremes with her."

"Went to extremes?"

"Had relations."

"I like that. If I make love to someone, that would be 'going to extremes.'"

"I may faint."

*   *   *

Jennie remembered the black residents of African Grove, a neighborhood bordered by Duane and Anthony Streets, near New York Hospital, where she had had occasion to be treated for injuries. A taboo had existed, though, on sex with black men. She felt that it would be more conspicuous for her to walk arm in arm with a black woman on the Bowery in 1895 than it had been to flounce alongside an Irish ruffian.

Jennie had arrived too late for the heyday of racially mixed, high-profile houses of prostitution and saloons, which had thrived in the Five Points neighborhood through much of the nineteenth century; by the 1880s, the black sex district, called African Broadway, ran along Seventh Avenue from Twenty-third Street to Fortieth. In addition to a highly vocal prostitution trade, African Broadway was home to the mixed-race "black and tans," interracial dance halls. Mostly run by black entrepreneurs whose majority-black businesses met with little interest by police, the black and tans, such as Digg's Hotel, Percy Brown's Café, and Nigger Johnson's dance house, were wildly popular nightspots, where blacks and whites danced together despite loud criticism from opponents of racial integration. At Baron Wilkins's Place, a favorite of the sporting class, the owner offered "a special room where white women and colored men can meet and be protected."[18]

*　　*　　*

"So," Jackman said, "Exactly where did you hang out, Jennie?"

"Besides the Bowery," Jennie said, and began to lift her fingers for numerical emphasis, "one, in the foreign Hebrew quarter: Grand, from Bowery eastward to Allen, and Allen and Christie, for several blocks on both sides of Grand; two, in the foreign Italian quarter, containing also a large sprinkling of Irish immigrants: Grand, from Bowery westward to Sullivan and Thompson, Bleecker from Thompson to Carmine, and Mulberry south of Spring; three, in Chinatown: Doyers, Pell, and Mott Streets. I did not seek the Chinese, but the adolescent toughs and young gentlemen libertines who visited Chinatown evenings . . ."

"The Chinese men weren't attractive to you?" Jackman asked.

"Oh, I knew better. I wasn't pretty enough for Chinese men.

"But back to the sports," Jennie said. "There were two entirely separate types who overlapped in the underworld. I wrote about them in my third book. Which was destroyed. But that is another story. No one will ever read my *Riddle of the Underworld*. The two types were the 'flash' types. Very, very obsessed with their appearance. Utterly conceited. The mirror was their best friend. They didn't care about anyone or anything. Terribly blasé. A thousand pleats along the placket of their shirts. Glittering rings on every finger. A perfumed pomade slicking their hair. Polished boots. Thick gold watch chains. They had manners but they seemed almost, you know, like manners that they had taught themselves."

"Like half the fellows I know!" Jackman erupted. "They madden me with their mispronunciations."

"And their fastidiousness never appealed to me. I find it, well, effeminate. These flash types were to be found on Broadway most nights, clacking along in their carriages, on the prowl but not wanting to appear that they cared. They'd make their way to the theater, to the 'third tier,' for the company of a whore. Dozens of whores stalked the theaters, even the most elegant theaters, looking for customers. They were quite open, quite popular."

"So you must have liked the other kind. Not the 'flash type,'" Jackman said.

"Oh, I did. I did. These were my Bowery boys. Young as sixteen or seventeen – which, in my defense, was my age the first time I dared to go out dressed as Jennie June. These, these *gods*, traveled in packs, and would approach a girl on her own with the enticement to join them for a drink, bring a friend. These were the men in the lowest of the low dive bars. Slat-walled, tar-floored, soot-covered hellholes. I spent so many nights . . ."

124

"Eventually, these men married. That was the truth. I applauded it. If you were a genuine, virile man, you found a wife and sired children. But it was hard to choose. There were personal ads in the newspapers, there were women whom you knew from society, from good families, who might abhor the sexual freedom you knew you'd continue to explore. The men I went to extremes with, I knew that eventually they'd get married . . ."

"You never wanted to marry them yourself?"

Jennie laughed. "The very idea!"

CHAPTER NINE

The three drunk gangsters met their young spy at the Clam House, a tunnel-shaped bar on 133rd Street, just after one in the morning. The Clam House attracted celebrities like the actress Tallulah Bankhead, the singer Libby Holman, and Princess Murat, the Parisian royal who'd had her eye on Mayme White. The signature performer at the bar was Gladys Bentley, all 250 pounds of her in top hat and tails, putting her own lurid, alto twist on popular bawdy songs.

The gangsters had started hanging out at the Clam House a few years back, when they'd noticed how fond fairies were of coming up to Harlem to meet men. They had spies from the fairy world moving through Harlem as easily as through the Village. The best spy, the handsomest, had been working the Faggots Ball all night, keeping a close watch on A'Lelia Walker, the heiress, and on that asshole Bo Weinberg, who wanted to move on her tonight.

The handsome spy had brought a frail young fairy with him, and he had his arm around the little thing. "You have to hold off on Walker," he said. "That old drag, Jennie June, set off alarms all over the Ball."

"You kiddin' me?" asked the least drunk of the gangsters.

"No, I'm not kidding you. You have to wait."

"Well, who the fuck is Jennie June?" asked the third gangster. "I never heard of her."

"A faggot warrior," the handsome spy said, shaking his head appreciatively. "You ought to see that creature."

The entertainer onstage stopped singing for a moment. "You'd better listen to me!" she shouted.

Ma Rainey, in a tight red dress, shook with pain onstage, her fists tight against her face, and she resumed singing "Sissy Man Blues":

> My man got a sissy, his name is "Miss Kate,"
> He shook that thing like jelly on a plate.

CHAPTER TEN

Richard Bruce Nugent shambled away from the dance floor; the thing about these *fuck*ing drag balls was how popular they'd gotten – you wanted to ask, who the fuck *are* you people? You spectators.

"Have a cigarette for a lady?" someone called to him.

He pulled the pack from his pocket and tossed it to the tall, red-speckled showgirl. "There ya go," he purred.

Six feet tall, his face "the color of a bleached saffron leaf . . . his hair wiry and untrained,"[19] Nugent was in the market for some muscular Latin masculinity, maybe costumed as a boxer, or Adonis – but he kept running into friends.

It hadn't surprised him to look up at A'Lelia's box seats and see Langston in a smart, slim suit. Langston had always been loyal to his messy friends, no matter how buttoned-up he kept himself.

Years ago, Bruce had met Langston at a party and they'd hit it off well, walked each other home, talking about art and life and people they knew in common. They both knew D.C., the society nonsense, though from different sides of the divide. Langston had, in his calm way, told Nugent that D.C. was about as bad a place as he'd ever lived. If you were too dark, if you did menial work, or if you hadn't graduated from college, they kept you at arm's length. They were like tacky rich people without being really rich. Once Langston had made it big, they tried to claim him as one of their own, but still they were rude to his mother, still they tried to impress him by talking about their ancestors, all that bullshit about how they were related to George Washington, "on the colored side."

Nugent, for his part, was part of the Washington society that Langston hated, and like anyone who grew up in a tight community – even if it was snobbish and foolish – he had absorbed plenty of its mores: the hyperawareness of skin color, the worries about being gay and how it might shame his family.

Nugent, who was a visual artist as well as a poet and prose writer, had a genius for provocation, but he wasn't as focused on "making it" as Langston was, and his career certainly hadn't followed the same rocket-launch trajectory as Langston's or Countee's (though it looked like Countee was sputtering, losing his voice by choking so hard on polite black bullshit.) Langston was a Knopf poet, a round-the-world traveler, written up in glamorous magazines like *Vanity Fair,* really Svengalied by nance cultural types like Carl Van Vechten and Alain Locke. He escorted the rich and famous to high-culture events, and even tonight, there he was, up in A'Lelia Walker's box while Nugent, openly gay, undisciplined, tieless, was down here with the people who lived in the life. Not that Nugent had regrets. Days were his own, and his nights, well, they were rich.

In 1926, Nugent had published "Smoke, Lilies and Jade," his most controversial work, in the only issue of *FIRE!!*, a journal he'd formed with Langston Hughes and the novelist Wallace Thurman. *FIRE!!* meant to be the Renaissance's equivalent of the experimental journals that were flourishing in Paris; it also meant to explicitly inflame the polite DuBois-influenced black writers who preferred the Renaissance's brightest to focus on the sociological and race-uplift themes that appeared in *The Crisis*. With the logo "Devoted to Younger Negro Artists" splashed across the front of its blazing red and black cover, *Fire!!* included bold contributions from Zora Neale Hurston, Hughes, and Thurman, but it was Nugent's piece that made explicit the homosexual context of the Renaissance. In "Smoke, Lilies and Jade," Nugent layers images of young muscular men, synesthetic metaphors, and deep sentiment with the names and places of his artistic circle. On the page, in

131

ellipse-heavy prose, Nugent connects Langston, Zora, Wally, and red calla lillies to "rounded buttocks" and a "graceful muscled neck."[20]

Four years had pased, and Nugent was as committed to the artist's life as he had ever been. He was going to hold on to what he had learned, keep creating. That little moment, the Harlem Renaissance – why did the leaders, the academics, the critics, want to embalm it? It lived; you just had to look for it; you just had to understand that not all of its artists sought publicity, or the approval of Carl Van Vechten.

He wanted to tell them all, Look, you can enjoy it without killing it. You really can.

Now he swayed into the crowd that he would later write about in an unpublished novel, *Geisha Man:* ". . . the dance floor was a single chaotic mass of color. Abbreviated ballet skirts of pink, blue, silver and white dancing with Arab shieks in fantastic colors . . . Turks with bright ballooned trousers, curled pointed boots and turbans with sweeps of brilliant feathers and sparkling glass gems . . . pirates in frayed trousers, bloody shirts, headbands, earrings and tattoos . . . houri girls . . . fashion girls . . . Apache Indian, Spanish, Dutch and Japanese girls. One man resplendent in the third-dynasty costume of a Chinese bandit king. Court dresses of Louis

XIV ... hula girls and boys ... clowns and deaths and pirouettes ... Indian temple dancers ... evening gowns and the black and white of full dress. Boys dressed as girls and simpering sadly. Girls dressed as boys and bulging in places. Corked clowns and stage takeoffs. A peacock gown with a train of iridescent green being broken if held and trampled if not. Flame kings and snow queens. Bathing beauties and Greek Gods . . ."[21]

In the novel's imaginative re-creation of the drag ball, Nugent impersonated an effeminate, masochistic Japanese man named Kondo Gale, who'd gotten his start as a geisha in Osaka. While dating a muscular, dominant man named Don, Kondo Gale dresses up in a silver gown sewn with hundreds of silver poppies – his costume for the ball. Consumed by fantasies of becoming a woman "in flowing silks and silver and colors always, with a modish mannish look and gestures," Kondo is approached on the dance floor by dozens of men whose remarks are "flattering in their very crudeness."[22]

Kondo dances with a "handsome Turk. He was whispering little exciting breaths in my ear and surreptitiously kissing me. The feel of his muscles! His thighs darted into the folds of silver poppies, connecting with electric simplicity ever so often through the metallic flowers. The body feel of him! I was floating on music and sensuality."[23]

Everywhere Kondo Gale turns, he sees ex-lovers who long for him, and it's all "a little too intense, a little too foolish, a little too painted. A little too unreal." After one more dance, Kondo Gale leaves with Gale, a macho international playboy he'd met back in Osaka whose name he shares. And with a burst of poetic insight, Kondo Gale confirms to the reader that Gale is his biological father.[24]

They drive "long cool miles into the country. Across a ferry. Long cool miles of damp leaves and darkness." When they arrive at Gale's country mansion, the playboy promises Kondo that he is "through with women" and they'll be married.[25]

The Grand March of Fairies had begun, and Nugent was trapped, jostled among the girls who floated slowly by, hands on hips, arms above their heads, waving, shrieking to the VIPs. They each had an elongated moment in the spotlight, where they did a turn, worked a few bits of magic on the runway. The MC pointed to each girl and the judges gauged the crowd's applause.

Damn Van Vechten, thought Nugent, watching as the judges fell into discussion. How does he end up holding court in every circle?

He's up there with six thousand pleats in his shirt, tinkly, shiny bracelets, more than Mayme White wears, and those teeth! His kisses must be something to see.

Nugent shuddered at the thought. You didn't want to stumble upon Carl Van Vechten naked in the arms of a young man, but these things happened. Carlo was an exception – he was one of the only whites with a name whom you'd run into at the sex parties along 133rd and 140th Street.

The man had an eye, a collector's eye. Nugent had to admit it – but so what? It certainly wasn't as textured as some other collectors Nugent knew. For instance, Alexander Gumby, in his lovely storefront salon, on Fifth Avenue between 131st and 132nd, brought an intense discipline to his collecting; Gumby, without half the fame of Van Vechten, had created an encyclopedia of black life, and the man lived it, he wasn't just a tourist.

Perhaps the difference, Nugent thought, was that Gumby, black and with the background of a butler, a bellhop, didn't try to make every aspect of the black experience an exotic bazaar. Or maybe it was just that Gumby was the beneficiary of a rich white banker man – a stockbroker, Charles W. Newman, whom he'd met in 1910 – and Van Vechten was always insinuating that *he* might be your patron if you were willing to pay the price.

Van Vechten was smart about dance and music. He published his fluffy books; hell, Nugent hadn't minded *Peter Whiffle*, one of the man's silliest. But Van Vechten had come from the middle of small-town America and now he sat on the dais, judging Harlem's parties. Well, Nugent chuckled to himself, at least he offered comedy, the way he mixed worlds. Harlem had laughed mirthlessly the time Fania Marinoff, Van Vechten's actress wife, tried to give Bessie Smith a farewell peck on the cheek after Bessie had had too much to drink.

Bessie shoulder-blocked the little woman, gave her one sharp, heavy swat, and shouted, "Get the fuck away from me. I ain't never heard of such shit!"

Nugent watched without surprise as the judges, clearly led by Van Vechten, awarded first prize to a man painted apple green, naked but for a glittering green thonged patch.

"Now we've been wondering among ourselves just *who* you are. I daresay I can't tell," Van Vechten asked the winner.

"I'm yours," the man said.

Nugent, shaking his head and laughing, shambled away, looking for a corner.

*   *   *

136

Nugent was about to smoke a panatela when who should come bumbling up to him but Langston, looking good enough to eat.

"Larkspurs and diamond lilies!" Langston shrilled, in deadly imitation of Carl Van Vechten.

Nugent about choked on his drag.

"Guess what?" Langston said, the sissy voice replaced by his everyday smoothness.

"What?"

"Lelia's having a party. I'm looking for you and Caska and, I guess, Harold. You see 'em?"

Nugent raised an eyebrow.

CHAPTER ELEVEN

A young woman with marcelled waves and diamond-and-gold earrings as big around as eggs stood in a corner near the grand staircase, pausing, a pen to her notebook, recording conversation as it swirled around her.

Another woman, this one white, stalked up to her and thrust a yellowing newspaper clipping in her hand. "What is your name?"

The first woman didn't look up when she said, "Excuse me?"

"Tell me your name!"

The first woman flipped her notebook shut and took the yellow paper from the white woman's hand.

"Are you Geraldyn Dismond?!" the white woman demanded.

"Why do you want to know?"

"Do you write for the *Inter-State Tattler?*"

"Why, yes I am. And yes I do."

The white woman smiled. "I just want to thank you. Your paper – this article – just earned me half a million dollars in court. If you'll give me your phone number, I'd like to take you out for a drink some evening?"

When the new divorcée had departed, clutching Geraldyn's card like a lucky rabbit's foot, Geraldyn finally unfolded the article, and immediately began to laugh. This had been one of her favorites a couple of years back. Smiling to herself, she read it through to the end:

Recently the chocolate drop press made a great racket over the story of a brown-skin frail who, claiming to have been the common-law wife of a white millionaire for seventeen years, appealed to the courts with a charge of abandonment and a request for an endowment of bucks . . . We discussed the incident with a girl friend of ours, whom we have always found to be a woman of unusual frankness, and her verdict, it seems to us, covers the whole problem with almost biblical brevity and at the same time reveals the true feminine attitude toward life. "If that woman hasn't feathered her nest in seventeen years," our friend declared, "she does not deserve a moment's sympathy."[26]

Geraldyn Dismond had left her husband, the radiologist Binga Dismond, at home tonight. As the society columnist for the *Inter-State Tattler*, she had to celebrate without him on many nights. It had been easier back in Chicago, where they'd met. He'd been track-star A-student Binga, and Geraldyn had been working her way up the newspaper business.

The Faggots Ball was just her first stop tonight. She'd heard that A'Lelia was throwing together a stampede at her apartment. It wasn't hard to picture how this one would go.

Geraldyn was happiest at A'Lelia's parties. She fiercely promoted A'Lelia in her columns, and she thought that her accounts of a few of the parties were among her best work.

Once, she had stopped dead in the middle of a column to write what she still thought was the defining word on A'Lelia's frenzied dos:

Some parties are given while others are thrown. The parties that are given are the ones you take your wife to, which obviously prevents you from getting in contact with a good time. Last Saturday evening . . . was the scene of the other kind of party – one that was thrown, pitched, tossed, heaved and catapulted . . . Was it wild? Well, Bacchus himself passed out before midnight and along about two o'clock the shade of Rabelais returned to its tomb with its head hanging low in defeat. Four bushels of vine leaves were swept out by the maids Sunday morning, and along with them the following rags, bones and hanks of hair."[27]

And then she had listed the names of A'Lelia's inner circle, the party girls, the witty boys, the bootleggers and gamblers, the sheiks, vamps, and man-eaters.

The frivolously sophisticated British poet, critic, essayist, and memoirist Sir Osbert Sitwell counted A'Lelia's 1926 debutante ball, held in her brownstone for two of her nieces, among the best parties he attended in New York. A'Lelia greeted him in a high-roofed tent room, highly ornamented in the Second Empire style. Flanked by her nieces, A'Lelia wore "an elephant-gray tight Greek ball dress" and her hair was braided with "a Greek fillet in gold."[28]

A'Lelia, as was her habit, retired to her bedroom suite right as the party began to get crowded, bringing Sitwell with her for a private chat. She popped two bottles of good champagne and confided that her feet hurt, that their soreness had ruined her first honeymoon, too.

Langston Hughes had heard similar stories, and once, in tears and half drunk, A'Lelia had shown Langston a gold shoehorn, which, she claimed, was all she had left of her first husband.

* * *

Years after her death, Carl Van Vechten kept A'Lelia's flame burning, telling everyone who wanted to write about New York in the 1920s that no portrait was complete without her. A'Lelia, like a more engaging Jay Gatsby, was on the sidelines during her parties – yet still she managed, in her absence, to be the center of deep speculation.

As Van Vechten wrote in a piece commissioned by *Vanity Fair* but never finished, A'Lelia, in her silks, furs, and jeweled headpieces, "looked like a queen and frequently acted like a tyrant."[29]

The town house on West 136th Street was luxurious, but for an out-and-out spectacle, nothing could match the parties at the huge mansion in Westchester.

Thirty-four rooms on the shore of the Hudson River, twenty miles north of Harlem in Irvington-on-Hudson, the Westchester mansion had been Madame Walker's intended home; she knew that she and A'Lelia would fight if they lived too close to one another. Surrounded by scions of America's aristocracy, from Astors to Rockefellers, designed by one of the first black architects to be licensed in New York, the estate was named Villa Lewaro by A'Lelia's friend Enrico Caruso, using, for emphasis, the first letters of Lelia Walker Robinson's first married name. With pale stucco, rouge tile roof, lavish gardens, subtle tapestry-covered walls, and coffered ceilings, Villa Lewaro cost $250,000 to build in 1918, just a year before Madame died.

Like the Great Gatsby himself, A'Lelia suffered from intense and persistent fears of being alone, so when she had to be in Westchester she brought Manhattan guests, bands, food, and booze with her.

These were long, lost weekends: The villa spotlit at night. The heavenly sound of a gently swinging band carrying across the Hudson.

Costumed, bewigged servants met guests outside for the formal arrival, but by midnight all decorum had gone out the window.

Blanche Dunn would be cheating on her latest rich lover, with a numbers man or a ferociously smart young Howard student. Nobody's thinking about the strapping boy's little librarian girlfriend off in the corner, crying. But after a while, after a few drinks, Miss Books might let a young sheik follow her into an empty bedroom. By midnight, the doors were all closed.

Downstairs, there'd be gin, whiskey, scotch, rye, bourbon, and beer bubbling freely, but for these massive blowouts, A'Lelia kept the best stock of champagne in a cupboard in her bedroom, and only the innermost circle was allowed to share.

Like a cat, A'Lelia longed to get comfortable, to be peaceful in a smaller, self-contained room. She'd have Mayme and a few more girls to wait on her. A man or two, whoever amused her at the moment, preferably one of the sissy boys, Carlo Van Vechten, or the gorgeous Harold Jackman, who'd bust her open, the way he mimicked everyone from downstairs at the party.

Harold was like Mayme. His engine never seemed to run out of gas. You turned your head at a party, and there he was, talking to someone new. Often a sleek pale English boy whose eyes welled with longing.

Harold knew that A'Lelia got bored easily, so he never bored her. Once, she'd gotten up to leave a party where there had been nothing but talk talk talk, New Negro this and W. E. B. DuBois and Alain Locke and not a lick of jazz. Jackman had taken her by the arm and said, about his boyfriend, "Countee loves 'talking parties.'" And that had broken her bad mood. They'd just sat there and made fun of Countee and eaten and drunk and enjoyed themselves.

At the end of these long nights, Mayme would help A'Lelia to bed, and they'd whisper good night.

The party raged on beneath them, spilling out into the lawn.

And in the morning, the gesture that Langston had always been enamored of, the pipe organ playing softly, so that sleep came to a soft end.

*   *   *

In winter, the rooms of her mansions and apartment were warm, but in the summer the heat was unbearable. Still, the dancing did not stop.

At their height in the twenties, her parties resembled wildly out-of-control stampedes, no rules, no ending point.

There were rumors of orgies, of impromptu drag parties.

As the Harlem dancer Mabel Hampton recalled, there were these "funny parties – there were men and women, straight and gay. They were kinds of orgies. Some people had clothes on, some didn't. People would hug and kiss on pillows and do anything they wanted to do. You could watch if you wanted to. Some came to watch, some came to play. You had to be cute and well-dressed to get in."[30]

But Geraldyn's favorite A'Lelia party was one she didn't quite believe had actually taken place. It sounded like something A'Lelia and her gang would do, so Geraldyn had repeated the story dozens of times that A'Lelia once threw an elaborate prank, a provocative play on race relations. She seated white guests in the kitchen and served them pig's feet, chitterlings, and bathtub gin. In the luxe parlor, she served black guests caviar, pheasant, and her special, bootleg-best champagne.

Geraldyn had the unfortunate habit of writing imaginary obituaries for larger-than-life figures. She'd edit and reedit them in her mind for years before the celebrity actually died.

She'd been thinking through A'Lelia's lately, after Binga had told her that A'Lelia looked sick, that A'Lelia was going to die a quick death, soon, just as her mother had.

Geraldyn was thinking something like, A'Lelia Walker had never thrown rent parties, those staples of working-class Harlem: too-too-terrible, too-*bad*, piano-banging, quarter-pint bathtub-gin fêtes, parties you threw if you lived uptown, if you were broke, if Mr. Landlord was due. A'Lelia Walker never threw rent parties, but no one held it against her. By all accounts the parties she threw were every bit as fierce, addictive, and arduous as those that the poor folks threw. Both in Westchester, where she owned the spectacular estate Villa Lewaro, and in lush-life Harlem, where she maintained twin limestone town houses and an opulent, compact apartment around the corner, Lelia gathered New Yorkers for her marathon nights.

Popping a cigarette in her mouth, Geraldyn could hardly wait to be sipping that fine champagne, kicking back on the plush sofa, music floating across the room. Even though the Westchester mansion was on the market, the twin town houses in Harlem were rented out to the New York Department of Health, and a rumor had spread that A'Lelia had merely borrowed the car that had driven her to the ball tonight, Geraldyn believed A'Lelia was more enmeshed in her business than anyone gave her credit for. So lush, so imperious, she still seemed to be living a gilded life, windows shut so you couldn't sense the depression raging outside.

It was, Geraldyn thought, a seductive place to pass a night.

CHAPTER TWELVE

"You know," Jennie said to Harold Jackman. They had taken their seats in Blanche Dunn's box, which Blanche had vacated, leaving for A'Lelia's impromptu party.

"You know," Jennie repeated, "the headquarters for drags used to be Paresis Hall, on Fourth Avenue several blocks south of Fourteenth Street."

"Was it this big?" Harold asked.

"Oh, no. Not at all. In front was a modest barroom; behind, a small beer garden. The two floors above were divided into small rooms for rent."

"Where's Caska?" Harold said. "I promised I'd wait for him – to go to A'Lelia's. Would you like to come?"

"Me, to A'Lelia Walker's? A bit like taking Joseph Merrick to the queen's, isn't it? First I am sitting in Blanche Dunn's box – and now you invite me to A'Lelia Walker's. Tonight I may just die. But a happy girl."

"But I interrupted you. Go on. Paresis Hall."

"It bore almost the worst reputation of any resort of New

149

York's underworld. Preachers in New York pulpits of the decade would thunder philippics against it. They fundamentally misunderstood the nature of the clientele. These were the upper classes, mixed with middle classes. Culturally and ethically, its distinctive clientele ranked high. Paresis Hall was never my own headquarters. I visited it only now and then. I wandered more widely, and in some respects flaunted my androgynism to a greater extent, than any other female impersonator of my day. I took greater chances than any other fairy, sexually, but I never appeared in public in female attire."

Jennie stopped to cough. "Excuse me."

"Would you like a drink? Some water?"

She shook her head and went on. "On one of my earliest visits to Paresis Hall – about January 1895 – I seated myself alone at one of the tables. I had only recently learned that it was the androgyne headquarters. Since nature had consigned me to that class, I was anxious to meet as many examples as possible. As I took my seat, I did not recognize a single acquaintance among the several score young bloods, soubrettes, and androgynes chatting and drinking in the beer garden. In a few minutes, three short, smooth-faced young men approached and introduced themselves as Roland Reeves, Manon Lescaut, and Prince Pansy – aliases, of course, because few refined androgynes would be so rash as to betray their legal name in the underworld."

"But you could tell they were fairies."

"Not only from their names, but also from their loud apparel, the timbre of their voices, their frail physiques, and their feminesque mannerisms."

"Feminesque?"

"Yes, don't you like that? Feminesque! Roland was the chief speaker. His trunk and legs were not so feminine, but he excelled in womanly features, with such marine-blue eyes and pink-peony cheeks as any woman. He was naturally beardless, too."

"What did he want from you?" Jackman asked.

"'Jennie June,' he said, 'I have seen you at the Hotel Comfort, but you were always engaged. A score of us have formed a little club, the Cercle Hermaphroditos. For we need to unite for defense against the world's bitter persecution of bisexuals. We care to admit only extreme types – such as like to doll themselves up in feminine finery. We sympathize with, but do not care to be intimate with, the mild types, some of whom you see here tonight even wearing a disgusting beard!"

"I don't know how to say this," Jackman started, "but those high-class fairies sound even more girlish than you. Don't take it the wrong way. I'm not trying to insult you."

"Oh, I was naturally as timid as the crybaby species of woman. I always promenaded the dimly lighted side streets of these immigrant slums with the light step of a cat crossing a road, ever alert, ever halting to recoinnoiter, and occasionally compelled to take to my heels on catching sight, a dozen yards away, of the burly shoulders and bristle-covered, defiant chin of a ruffian who never cared for me, but who, because of his innate loathing of fairies, which, of course, was nurtured by the statutes on the books, beat and robbed me at every opportunity. Though I was as swift of foot as a gazelle, he would, still, sometimes catch me. I could tell that my fear was a strong aphrodisiac for him; I could tell that he loved for me to beg.

"'Please,' I would say. And he would hit me, lightly at first, as if teasing me.

"And then would come a sledgehammer blow to my face, or my chest.

"I would pretend that his strength had knocked me quite unconscious.

"It pleased his vanity to believe he was that strong."

"And he was that stupid!" Jackman said.

"Well, and that! Have you heard of the fainting goats?" Jennie asked.

Jackman shook his head.

"They are from Tennessee. You used to see them in the sideshow. They have enormous eyes, bulging eyes. And when they are startled, their legs lock and they fall over on their sides, unconscious. My brothers used to love to see them, and scare them, and make them fall over. I think for them there was an immense feeling of power, to raise their boy arms to the goat and see the goat fall. That was how a certain kind of ruffian behaved toward fairies. It seemed to be programmed in their brains, in their souls. On sight they wanted to erase us."

Jackman found himself longing for an escape. He wished he had gone to the Clam House, where the freaky queers seemed so happy. A minute with some soft boy, dancing hard to some twisted blues song.

Jennie asked for one of Jackman's cigarettes now, and took a deep rasping drag. "Is it any wonder that before I started out of my home for a ramble in the Bowery, or in Hell's Kitchen, I felt as if I were going forth to meet death on the scaffold? I made a pact with myself, every time I felt the blood rush to the surface of my forehead: this will be the last time. No more after tonight. I felt like a soldier about to embark on a great battle from which he might never come back alive. As I transformed myself from mild Earl Lind into effervescent Jennie June, I would sing to myself, "Why oh why should we be melancholy, boys / Whose business 'tis to die?"

She went on. "But I was fascinated by the men who spent all their time on these streets, and I was haunted by memories of the ones who had already given me the pleasures of their company, and I wanted so badly to meet them again. In my bed, beneath my sheets, eyes closed, I would imagine I could feel their firm torsos pressing against me, telling me what they wanted me to do for them. And once I had had one of them, I wanted more."

"More!" Jackman laughed. "You had the hunger, didn't you?"

"I had a craze for as many as possible. *Maximum erat octo; modus, duo aut tres.* Once I was downtown, there was no reason to stop. Success bred success."

"Eight? Eight! In a row? At once?"

Jennie merely smiled.

"Oh, I never learned my lesson," she said finally. "One night I encountered four stalwart artillerymen of about my own age. I was bewitched and I had to find some way to make their acquaintance immediately. I could not take the risk of indecently accosting them as girls commonly did."

"So what did you do?"

"I walked along right under their noses on the crowded

154

sidewalk, making myself impossible to ignore. I swayed my tiny shoulders energetically and took tiny little steps."

Jackman clapped his hand over his forehead. "You just minced past them, in the middle of the street, and thought you were less conspicuous than if you had solicited them the way the prostitutes did? You really did?"

"I wish you wouldn't make me feel sad about myself as I am telling a story. I am enslaved by your magnificent and masculine beauty, but still . . ."

"Oh, go on."

"In a few seconds, the artillerymen shouted out, 'What kind of pretty do we have here?' They surrounded me and for several delicious minutes they overwhelmed me with terms of endearment."

"And you were just stoic, huh?"

"I begged them to take me to be their baby and slave."

"Of course."

"A room was secured for an hour. When the time came to part, I was pained at the thought. Oh, it was impossible to possess for an hour the society of human demigods whom one would like to abide with and worship forever, and then to be abruptly, completely, and eternally separated. It was an empty feeling, a catastrophe.

When we were back on the Bowery, they repeatedly asked

me to leave them. I lingered on their periphery, attempting to appear desirable to them, but when we arrived at a dance hall that had been their first destination, they were compelled to use threats of violence. My soldiers left me at the door. Two flash adolescents emerged at that very moment. The youths paused in my vicinity to light cigarettes – "

"Ah," Jackman said, "wonderful idea." He lit up.

"The sports had no matches. Of course, I always carry a pack."

"Of course you do! Even though you don't smoke."

"'May I light them for you?' I asked in a babyish voice, letting one shoulder droop ever so slightly. 'You are such handsome fellows. I cannot tell you how much I adore you.'

"'What's here,' the taller of the two says genially. 'A fairy?'

"'Yes, I'm a fairy, and I would like to be a slave to a sport like you. Like both of you. You look every inch like two sluggers. How I worship sluggers!'

"The talkative sport grinned. 'What do you see in a boy to love? I don't see anything. What good do you get out of loving a fellow?'

"'Well, what do you see in a girl to love? I don't see anything at all. Girls are not brave. They are not rough. They are not strong. You are brave, rough, and strong, and that is why I love you. The weak love the strong and the strong, the weak. The brave love the timid and the timid, the brave. The shy love the bold and the bold, the shy.'

"The sports took me to an alley. They announced that they were detectives and would arrest me for accosting them unless I gave up everything I had.

"I had less than a dollar.

"'I don't know whether to lock you up or give you a thrashing, you dickless fairy!' the sport shouted.

"'Please let me go! I am very weak and can't stand much pain,' I said, though of course I had in my life stood terrible beatings, from gorgeous men such as this sport. 'You want to punish me for being a fairy, but I can't help being what Nature made me. Do you think anyone would be a fairy from choice when they are the most despised of mankind? Think how much better God has been to you than to me. Have pity on me! I am one of the most unfortunate of human beings! For your dear mother's sake – whom every boy must love – I beg you to show me mercy!'

"An appeal to mother love seldom failed."

Jackman applauded. "Good job! Excellent. You saved yourself, one more time."

*   *   *

"Oh, the nightclubs were where I first met my peers. One damp evening in 1897 I was in the company of a giant ruffian whom I had met on the Bowery."

"Oh, tell us!" It was Caska, bearing three glasses of whiskey and smiling broadly. "You seem to have captured my friend here. Is it Jennie?"

Jennie barely acknowledged the newcomer, and continued. "This tall, massive-shouldered man was seated on a hydrant just past the Bowery. I began my prattle and we soon walked off together. He had the look of such a reckless character that I was afraid to go somewhere private. He had that look in his eyes."

"Do you know that look, Harold?" Caska interrupted. "Have you seen it – lately?"

"May I *finish*?"

"Oh, by all means."

"We were soon joined by two of the giant's pals, who had come along to see what was up, because maybe there was a chance for highway robbery. But they discovered it was only a low-class fairy."

"Low class?" Jackman objected.

"Well, he didn't step out in all his jewels."

"Oh, of course not."

"May. I. Go. On?" Jennie asked. "These two pals were also the most splendid specimens of the youthful ruffian. I was

158

insane with desire for all three, and I simply reclined in the bosom of one, and now in the bosom of another, and I gave utterance to –"

"You gave utterance!" Caska said.

"I gave utterance to the infant's natural language expressive of contentment at being petted and babied by these giants, whom I affectionately called my 'Big Braves.' I would lift their hands to my mouth and cover them with kisses, and roll up their sleeves and cover their arms with kisses."

"So you're not the only one, Caska!" Jackman laughed.

Jennie smiled. "May I have a sip of whiskey?"

"I brought you a glass," Caska smiled.

Jennie sipped and whispered, "Thank you."

"Now you've had your drink, go on."

"After some time, two of them said good night, leaving me alone with the giant whose acquaintance I had first made. I finally agreed to accompany him to his room. Whenever we sighted a policeman, he remarked: 'Let's go over to the other side of the street. I don't want that cop to see my face.' After entering the side door of a repulsive-looking 'saloon,' we walked down a very long passage, divided into sections by several heavily barricaded doors, each provided with a peephole and door tender, who opened only to the elect. Protection was thus secured against surprises by the police.

We finally arrived in a spacious room filled with small tables, around which were seated a dozen flashily dressed 'sports,' about the same number of shabbily clad ruffians, three or four girls costumed as for a fancy-dress ball, and five 'sports,' in the biological sense of that word, that is, youths with no front teeth, hair *à la mode de* Oscar Wilde (that is, hanging down in ringlets over the ears and collar) and clad in bright-colored wrappers. Their faces were painted, and their bodies also were seen to be when later they threw aside the loose wrappers.

"The assemblage were sipping their favorite beverages. From time to time decidedly obscene dances took place. One of the painted youths furnished the dance music. Another from time to time rendered the latest songs in a treble voice.

"When some came forward to make my acquaintance; my friend introduced me as 'Miss June'; I protested: 'Not Miss June. That doesn't sound pretty. Jennie June. I am only a baby girl, not a grown-up female.'

"Three of the fairies were introduced to me as Jersey Lily, Annie Laurie, and Grace Darling. Two others had adopted the names of living star actresses. They were the unreflecting and uneducated victims of innate androgynism, and having passed their lives exclusively in the slums of New York, they had always been perfectly satisfied with the lot Nature had ordained for them . . . In unenlightened lands, as India, these human 'sports,' clad in feminine apparel, appear in public in the company of young bloods. Among the American Indians, they adopt the dress and occupation of a squaw, become married to a brave, and lead a quiet virtuous life of toil. But Christendom has refused to acknowledge that God has created this type of human being, the woman with masculine genitals. It hunts them down, and drives them from one section of our great cities to another by repeated raids on their resorts. It attributes their fundamental peculiarities to moral degradation, when they are due to Nature. Of course, in the case of these fairies in the slums of New York, deep moral degradation had supervened upon their innate androgynism.

"Active pederasts, who frequent such resorts, and normal young men who visit them to see life, spoon with me. A charming, smooth-spoken young gallant holds me on his lap before the roomful of people, and addresses me as 'My dear boy,' to which I reply, 'Please don't call me boy; call me girl. I am bewitched by my wooer, who uses with me the most indecent language I ever heard, and right in the hearing of all those assembled. I do not act rational. I do not wish to act rational. I wish to act like a baby girl. I am in high spirits, and the men visitors are much amused at my conduct. The other fairies also impersonate the woman and the baby, much to the amusement of their audience. Whoever has visited such a performance must acknowledge that this type of human being are born actors, or actresses, whichever term may be preferred. They themselves prefer the latter."

"I have an admission to make, to both of you," Jennie said.

"Please go ahead," Caska said, barely hiding his smirk.

"We were not very progressive. I will admit that. We would be sitting on the street corner in the Bowery, and we would sing from plantation songbooks. Do you know 'Old Black Joe'?"

"Do tell us," Caska said. "Sing it for us. We want you to."

"Gone are my friends / from the cotton fields away . . ."

"Okay, that will be enough," Jackman said quietly.

"Where are the hearts," Jennie continued shrilly, "Once so happy and so free / The children so dear / That I held upon my knee / Gone to the shore / Where my soul has longed to go / I hear their gentle voices calling: Old Black Joe."

Caska applauded with exaggerated passion.

"Stop, Caska."

"So tell us the worst," Caska said. "What is the worst thing that happened to you?"

"I don't know if I want to," Jennie said.

"We should really get going," Jackman said.

"Well, let me tell you the worst then. Before we're on our way."

"I had decided to try my luck in the Fourteenth Street theater district, which was at that time a favorite promenade of fairies.

"One evening I clad myself so as to present the most attractive appearance possible: a blue suit, with box-plaited, belted coat (Norfolk style); dark red necktie; white gloves; and patent-leather shoes. As a high-class fairy, I sought to dress in a distinctive manner, so as to be more readily recognized by my prey. Therefore unusually large neck bows and white gloves. Fairies are inclined to be loud in their dress. The excessive wearing of gloves and the wearing of a red necktie are almost universal with high-class fairies. Once a blackmailer to whom I would not hand out the three dollars demanded made good his threat to turn me over to a policeman, who took my red tie as conclusive evidence that I was a fairy. Of a fairy who was arrested for accosting on the street, I have heard it said: 'He got thirty days for wearing a red tie.'

"On my first visit to the theater district named, I promenaded up and down for about an hour, afraid to accost any adolescent.

"Finally one accosted me: 'How's business?'

"I was instantly in love with him.

"Arrived in his room, he treated me with marvelous gallantry, as if I had been a queen. For several weeks, I spent evenings in his company. He introduced me to his companions, they to theirs in turn, and before long I numbered among my acquaintances scores of the habitués of the gambling halls and other dens of vice of this quarter of the city, and associated with them in these places, though fellatio and coquetry were my own only departures from a most puritanical life. Such an environment was it that fate had in store for the innocent stripling of a few years before who had chosen for himself the self-abnegating career of a foreign missionary . . .

"Soon, all classes of sporting men – young actors, professional gamblers, racetrack bookmakers, and adolescents of some means and without occupation other than to sip continually of all the gross pleasures of life – constituted the associates of Jennie June during the following year and a half. I read in the newspaper several times that one of my paramours held a world's record in one branch of sport. I found that very few of this moneyed sporting class cared to go beyond joking with me and teasing me, and none beyond the age of twenty-five ever went to extremes. In this neighborhood at that time female *filles de joie* were numerous, and the sporting men were more than satiated. The fairy's success, of course, is inversely proportional to unmarried adolescents' opportunities with the gentle sex.

"During this period of my career, I learned that fairies are maintained in some public houses of the better class, and met several of these refined professionals, who resembled myself both physically and psychically. They commonly have plates substituted for their front teeth. Even I took this expedient under consideration. It was suggested to me to become an inmate of such a house, but I could make the career of a *fille de joie* only a side issue. I gave first place to the intellectual and others of the highest aims of life. My sister courtesans, both male and female, thought only of the sensual, and had adopted their occupation as a gainful one, whereas I sought merely the satisfaction of strong instincts, which unsatisfied would make practically impossible the higher life I regularly lived.

"During this period I knowingly encountered the first case of gonorrhea in a companion. So far as I know, I did not contract gonorrhea until 1917, after twenty-four years of promiscuity.

"But venereal disease was not at all the worst that happened. Not by a long shot. With the expansion of leisure time, those who hated fairies grew more resourceful, more ingenious in punishing us."

Caska and Jackman were silent, watching her with deep frowns.

"In Stuyvesant Square, young men stuck pins into me, inflicted slight burns with lighted matches, and pinched me unmercifully, particularly my penis. It seems that the higher the public standard of morality of adolescents, the greater the physical violence that they inflict on fairies."

"I absolutely believe that," Caska said.

"Later that same year, I picked up a boy on Fourteenth Street. He'd been with friends, but he asked me to accompany him to his room alone and I happily obliged. As we walked he kept hugging me close to him and saying excitedly how delicate I was."

"Uh-oh," Jackman said.

"A few minutes after we arrived in the young man's quarters in a furnished-room house, the other five friends burst in. They proved to be as heartless a gang as I had ever met, although belonging to the prosperous class of society. *Micturiverunt super meis vestibus atque me coegerunt facere rem mihi horribilissimam (balnam ani cum lingua, non aliter quam meretrices faciunt). Me coegerunt recipere tres eodem tempore, fellation, paedicatio, atque manustupratio. Ultimum mihi imperatum cum adolescnes non potuit facere inter femora eodem tempore.*"

"Slow it down," Caska said, "slow it down. My Latin's rusty."

"Don't make him," Jackman said. "Just let him speak, Caska. I am asking you, please. They raped him."

Jennie found herself stuttering, stopping and starting, thick tears choking her as she continued, "Later, one who had difficulty in achieving the desired results *me coegit ad fellationem unam semihoram* continuously, repeatedly punching me in the head and face because I did not do better by him. Again for a half hour continuously *me coegerunt ut supinum cubem atque usi erunt ore meo sicuti cunno, sic me strangulantes horribiliter. Cum priapus concurreret meas dentes*, they would punch me in the face, *atque mandabant ut desisterem eos mordere*."

"Their lechery finally sated," she rasped, "they shoved a red handkerchief into my mouth, and said: 'Do you know you are worse than a hog? You dickless fairy, going around to corrupt young fellows! We will teach you to keep away from Fourteenth Street hereafter!'"

"They weren't finished with you?" Caska whispered. He reached across the aisle to take Jennie's hand.

"I was conducted to a dark, deserted street, where one of them rained violent blows on my face, while I did nothing except to seek to protect my features as much as possible with my hands. Finally it occurred to me to feign unconsciousness. I played dead, and only then did they all hurry away."

CHAPTER THIRTEEN

By the time she was perceived as America's first black female millionaire, A'Lelia's mother knew better than to throw a cut-rate party. Whether she was entertaining political leaders back in Indianapolis or throwing lavish pageants at the mansion on the banks of the Hudson River, Madame's celebrations were extensions of the same pragmatic vision that had driven sales of hair products and kept hair salons and beauty colleges busy. Nothing was left to chance; no "insignificant" detail was overlooked. If she could have, she'd have written scripts for every guest. *You will have a good time – on my terms.*

It was no surprise to anyone that Madame always stood where all eyes could linger on her, on her poise, her impeccable clothes, the important men who stood, as if posed, beside her.

As A'Lelia sat in the Lincoln for the short ride to the apartment on Edgecombe Avenue, where she'd invited a dozen friends, she remembered the transfiguring experience of attending, as guest of honor, the party her mother threw in Indianapolis in the spring of 1914. She'd been visiting from New York, and when she entered the grand, crowded hall she felt like royalty at a coronation.

She experienced a stuttering gold vision: the room was gilded and immaculate; the men wore cutaway coats and the women seemed to glide in their pale gowns, all rustling silk, fragile as the swaying palms potted along the perimeter of the dance floor. A shower of white rose petals fell in her path as she walked up the stairs to the dais where Madame waited.

She caught sight of her hair in a mirrored wall panel and had to stop herself from gasping. The pearls laced through her hair in a meticulous stipple-stitch twinkled and glowed, reflecting light from the chandeliers that seemed to kaleidoscope above her. For an excruciating moment she thought she might faint, poised there, the heiress apparent. Like her mother, she wore a white dress, one of a kind, embroidered with gold thread.

"Welcome, everyone," Madame said proudly. "And most of all, I wish to welcome my daughter, Lelia."

As the string quartet played, A'Lelia took her mother's hands and clasped them in her own. "Thank you. I'm so happy to be here." It felt safer, somehow, to be thanking her mother in front of this elegant crowd. No one was going to be angry with her. No one could put her down. There was something punishing about being up here in the public eye, but the roar of it, the velocity, obliterated most of her fearfulness. Could she love her mother more than she did at this moment, both of them so beautifully dressed, the object of so much attention?

We are both extraordinary people, A'Lelia told herself. We've left St. Louis behind, haven't we?

Haven't we?

She felt certain that she would never know the ordinary world again.

"Listen," Madame was whispering to her. "Listen."

"Okay, I'm listening."

A'Lelia watched with the rest of the guests as a sleek woman in white chiffon joined them on the dais, shook Madame's hand and then took her place at an ornate podium at the front of the stage.

With her perfectly rounded O's and artillery-crisp T's, the woman was clearly a professional elocutionist, and A'Lelia prepared herself for a dull testimonial.

Instead, the woman recited a Paul Laurence Dunbar poem – and by the time she had finished the first line, the swank crowd began to smile broadly and then laugh.

"Dey had a gread big pahty," she began, her voice carrying in clear waves across the glittering ballroom, "down to Tom's de othah night . . ."

*   *   *

171

No matter how many times she stood on a stage next to Madame, whether it was for the Walker Manufacturing Company's annual conferences or the extravagant two-week open house that they hosted in February 1919 for Harlem infantrymen returning from Europe in World War I, A'Lelia would still get that knock-down feeling of Luck, capital L Luck, Lucky Me. As much as they fought over money, over A'Lelia's husbands, over A'Lelia's health and her dedication to the company, A'Lelia never stopped believing in her mother's genius. Madame was just indisputably a leader.

And A'Lelia wasn't. When Madame died, just months after she'd opened her Westchester mansion to the returning troops, a piece of A'Lelia – the scrubwoman's daughter – died with her. Never again would she feel lucky; Walker Manufacturing was *her* company, and as far as she was concerned, she was entitled to all of its profits.

Mr. Ransom, A'Lelia's business manager, had for years thought that A'Lelia might be the thrifty Walker; he used to ask her to be a tempering influence on her mother. But once Madame died, he knew that A'Lelia just might take the company down with her spendthrift ways.

A'Lelia's argument was that she spent money on lavish parties and luxe clothes and designer furniture because her home and party life and public appearance were an enormous part of the Walker Co. brand. She knew – as her mother had – that customers bought this lifestyle. If A'Lelia lived the life her customers aspired to, and if the national Walker sales force, on a more modest scale, was as committed to looking good, if every woman associated with the company was driven, vivacious, and well-spoken, then the Walker brand, and all its blessings, would remain in ascension. Her sycophantic, flattering courtiers – the ladies in waiting, the effeminate men, her crowd – certainly agreed with her. And an echo chamber only tells you what you want to hear.

On purely business terms, A'Lelia's most successful party was the extravagant wedding she threw for her adopted daughter, Fairy Mae Bryant, in November 1923.

Fairy was a tiny young woman with long, shiny, luscious hair that made a spectacular advertisement for the Walker hair products. When A'Lelia adopted her in 1912, she promised Fairy's mother she would ensure that Fairy received an excellent education. A'Lelia, as well as Madame Walker, saw the marketing potential of putting a "daughter" in the Walker advertisements, but their financial guru, Mr. Ransom, warned them that any implication that Fairy was Madame Walker's blood granddaughter would be advertising fraud.[31]

The wedding was repeatedly referred to in the press as

Harlem society's "million-dollar" ceremony, but A'Lelia privately bragged that the wedding had cost less than fifty thousand dollars, and was a spectacular investment in publicity.

A'Lelia didn't seem to care that Mae had not dreamed of being the wife of the older man with whom she'd been matched. A'Lelia – in unconscious imitation of her mother – was intent on micromanaging every aspect of the ceremony. She sent nine thousand invitations to friends, acquaintances, and notable business and political leaders from across the country and faraway lands.

On the morning of the wedding, thousands of curious people gathered outside the Harlem church. Bridesmaids were members of the Debutante Club that A'Lelia had started for Mae. A'Lelia, in a gold metallic gown from Paris, beamed, while Fairy Mae, in a headpiece that had been modeled after images from King Tut's tomb, sulked amid the splendor.

Once she began to throw parties, she didn't know how to stop, really; they were expected of her; her invitations brought invitations in kind. If she stopped, she might have to stay home, alone – everyone she'd ever loved had left her; her party friends were, at least, reliable.

Melancholia, impulsiveness, hostility, susceptibility to every slight – these chinks in A'Lelia's armor of wealth and style gave her parties their reckless edge. When money was low, she'd take it from the Walker salon's account – Mr. Ransom be damned. She would never give up. What did he expect her to do – move to Indiana for the rest of her life, stop traveling, stop wearing lovely clothes?

She sent out too many invitations, so she had too many guests. She provided too much alcohol in far too many varieties, so everyone drank far too much. She provided a groaning board of lavish meats, candies, and caviar, and she hated for the food to run out. She never, never sent her guests home, but simply retired to her bedroom with a select group of friends, as the party raged on in her home. She attracted first and foremost people who didn't stand on decorum – whether they were European royalty, Broadway stars, musicians, artists, writers, or freaks, all had to run the gauntlet, force their way through the dancing crowds. A committed partygoer had to arrive early, or risk not getting past the front door.

And once you were in, it might be all night before you'd find your way out.

A'Lelia's "signature" party was her least successful. Lore of the Harlem Renaissance revered the salon she began for the writers and artists of the Harlem Renaissance, the "Dark Tower." Nineteen-twenty-eight. The walls of her luxurious parlor were decorated with poems by the opposite camps in the Renaissance. Painted on one wall was the Langston Hughes poem "The Weary Blues," which celebrated with precision an aspect of the Renaissance that the upper crust tended to ignore – an old black man in a dimly lit club, playing the songs that had never been committed to words.

On the opposite wall was an essay excerpt by Countee Cullen, Langston's fading rival and spurned suitor.

A'Lelia's salon premiered in a cultural milieu that was every bit as fussily watched over as Proust's "faithful." Cullen, one of the Renaissance's fussiest poets, had written an analysis of black cultural expectations that narrowed the world that the black writer could explore.

Countee argued that the black audience abhors protagonists who are comic farmhands or domestics. The black audience also dislikes the snobbish professional class who look down on farmhands and domestics. He argued that too much bad grammar, dialect, and "Negro flavor" would alienate the black audience, as would too little common sense. He argued that the main character of a piece targeting the black audience must have achieved an exact measure of modest professional success – and be neither too rich nor too poor, for fear of offending the black audience. It would be best, he argued, if the protagonist owned a small business that caters to but does not exploit the black community. "Unless well-motivated," he argued, a black hero or heroine "will be frowned upon at once" if he or she breaks into song.[32]

So it was clearly impossible for A'Lelia to please her intended audience, who had such differing ideas of this Renaissance she hoped to celebrate. No matter what she did, a slim faction accused her of social climbing.

Even those she thought were dear friends. Vagabond bon vivant types like Richard Bruce Nugent, who wrote that she

had made her bid for space on the upper rungs of the sepia social-ladder, a bid which had been rejected by the securely-familied "lily-whites" of Washington, Philadelphia, Boston and points South, East and North; after she had decided fatalistically to make the best (and a much more amusing best it was) of the entertainment and looser sporting strata, she decided to become . . . a patron of the arts . . . Artists and their close associates had entrée into the tiny closed circles which refused the ambitious A'Lelia. Should she make herself their friend (and bountiful provider) it was more than conceivable that they might in turn leave the sacred doors a little ajar, or perhaps even go so far as to become active about casually sponsoring her among their friends in the restricted groups. For A'Lelia had not been able to accept quite her social failure . . .

"The Dark Tower," Nugent continued,

was named after a column in "Opportunity" Magazine conducted by Countee Cullen . . . She dedicated a floor of her mansion (the one on 136th Street in Harlem) to the enterprise. The large elaborately-floored room that overlooked the back garden.

. . . The place was to be completely informal – a quite homey, comfortable place to which [young artists] could bring their friends for a chat and a glass of lemonade, coffee or tea. Yet it was to have enough quiet dignity to impart weight to the poetry evenings and other gatherings which would, of course, take place there. From time to time there were to be hung on the walls of the room, with no ballyhoo, the pictures, etchings, and other works of the struggling artists. It was all to be quite Utopian . . .

. . . Finally the artists (and everyone else) received notice that the Tower was opening. This came as somewhat of a surprise to the planning committee who had thought that they were working with A'Lelia.

. . . Those engraved invitiations should have warned them, but blithely and blindly they attended, one and all. The large house was lighted brilliantly. There was an air of formality which almost intimidated them . . . the place was filled to overflowing with whites from downtown who had come up expecting that this was a new and hot nightclub. One by one the artists made their uncertain way toward the kitchen. At least they could eat. There was something leveling and comforting about eating. Then they saw the menus . . .

. . . Prices remained out of reach of most of the people for whom the place had been conceived and brought into being.

The New Negro made one or two loyal attempts to try to support the place, the misplaced idea of the place, but they could not afford it . . .[33]

Despite the salon's intended "informality," the mansion was still fit for A'Lelia. There were Aubusson carpets, lavender satin walls, massive Louis XIV furniture, a Sèvres tea service made of turquoise and amethyst paste, a pale blue Victrola, a baby grand piano, and regular performances by Broadway stars and nightclub singers.

The Dark Tower was a fashion showcase, with blacks and

whites showing off to one another. Bon vivant novelist Max Ewing described one evening to his parents in Ohio: "You have never seen such clothes as millionaire Negroes get into. They are more gorgeous than a Ziegfeld finale."[34]

But the Dark Tower came at a time when A'Lelia's money had begun to run low. After one NAACP benefit, when most of the grand folks came to the Dark Tower for an afterparty, A'Lelia socked one of her friends in the jaw when he tried to enter without paying the fifty cents admission charge. In letters to her financial advisor, A'Lelia promised that she had stopped throwing parties, and that if she was throwing parties, she certainly wasn't misappropriating any Walker Manufacturing money. In fact, she wrote to Mr. Ransom, the Dark Tower had been planned as a moneymaking club to be run by her adopted daughter, Fairy Mae.

She was desperate. She was lying. And the Dark Tower, as some grand salon, died from lack of interest. It lived on as shorthand, a vivid nickname for all the parties she threw at the twin limestone mansions.

Outside the Manhattan Casino, girls staggered into the cold night air in twos and threes, leaning into one another for warmth and company. The Faggots Ball had come to an end, but there'd be another one next year.

Suddenly, there was the rap rap rap of knuckles on the window and A'Lelia gasped, "Oh!"

But they were friendly faces. Langston. Mayme. And the police officer, the one who'd seen Dutch Schultz's kidnapping list.

A'Lelia rolled her window down. "Officer," she said, "would you like to attend a party this evening?"

He smiled. "I'll see you to your door, Mrs. Walker."

"Oh, no one stops at the threshhold of A'Lelia's door," Langston said.

"Get in, young men," Mayme ordered, and with a flourish of bracelets she scooted across the seat toward A'Lelia.

As the driver started up the car, A'Lelia vowed to make tonight's party one of her best. They usually were the ones she remembered best, these informal, private fêtes at the apartment around the corner, 80 Edgecombe Avenue, Number 21.

Her collection of elephants in precious materials. Rose and green taffeta falling elegantly from the ceiling.

She would call up a pianist, a singer.

Her bootlegger had already dropped by with a fresh supply.

"Are we ready, Mayme?" she asked.

Her friend took her hand and gently squeezed it.

"Good. Driver, let's go."

CHAPTER FOURTEEN

Jennie June had needed a breath of fresh air, so she told the two young men, Caska and Harold, that she would meet them outside, on the sidewalk in front of the Manhattan Casino, where she'd just had one of her best sprees in a good ten years.

A gruff voice from behind her said, "Excuse me, Jennie?"

"Yes?" she said, and as she began to turn she realized that a terrible end awaited her.

Two men she knew to be gangsters flanked her. With ruthless efficiency, they pushed her a step at a time toward a dark Lincoln Special. The door flew open, and she fell into the backseat.

"No!" she shouted. "Help me! No!"

The door slammed shut.

"Enough," a man whispered from beside her on the backseat. "Dutch Schultz asked me to see you home, Jennie."

She tried to scream through his palm, which held her mouth in a deadly muffle.

Help. Help.

She watched through the dark windows as Caska and Harold came out from the Ball, stopped, and looked up and down the sidewalk to find her.

"Driver, move on," her captor said, and the Lincoln sped off, disappearing with Jennie June into the night.

CHAPTER FIFTEEN

They decided that Jennie June had gone home.

"She frightened me, I've got to say," Jackman said. "I liked her. I did like her. But she frightened me."

"She didn't frighten *me*," Caska said. "But her *life* certainly did."

"Well put."

"Shall we just go to Clinton's?" Caska asked.

"A'Lelia's expecting us," Jackman said.

"Well, let's stop at Clinton's first, and if it's dull we'll hoof it to A'Lelia's."

"You've convinced me."

When they arrived at Clinton Moore's apartment, the party had already achieved its host's signature swank mellowness, with musky undertones, of course.

Clinton, famous for his sensual get-togethers, greeted them with tumblers of whiskey on the rocks.

A half-dozen men stood around the baby grand, listening to an impossibly handsome slim young man, Joey, singing, "Don't want my Manny / I don't need a friend . . ."

Another few men lounged on a deep couch, and many more lay in comfort on thick floor cushions. In every corner there were scarf-covered tables topped by Ming bowls of cut flowers.

Harold left Caska talking with a new boy in town, Fred or Ed, something like that, a short dark-haired white boy with those blue eyes, and wandered into the next room. A Hindu sarong lay open the length of the floor, surrounded by pillows, and a buffet of cheese and cold cuts, chopped vegetables, nuts, and mints was arranged for easy eating. When he reached for a cashew, a dark hand gently took his and helped the cashew find Harold's mouth.

The gesture was so familiar, he almost thought it was Countee, come home from Paris.

"Do I know you?" he asked the man, who held him, from behind, in a loose embrace.

"You will soon."

CHAPTER SIXTEEN

A year and a half later, A'Lelia found herself in need of the ocean's therapeutic charms. It was August 1931, and New York City was too hot.

She'd always been fond of Atlantic City, whose amusements had kept pace with New York's. Nightclubs, bootleggers, card gambling, and fine restaurants. With nearly half the population black, there were still segregated beaches, hotels, and nightclubs, but A'Lelia knew enough of the right people to make her way as she pleased. It didn't hurt that she had friends there who loved her to visit. She had found the Lincoln Apartment Hotel, just north of the boardwalk on Indiana Avenue, to be a gracious vacation spot. It was, back in the twenties, the world's largest fireproof hotel for black people, with 142 rooms and apartments.

Mayme, too, loved the ocean. Growing up in Philadelphia, she was only hours from the beach. Her father, in fact, had helped to build a town just south of Atlantic City, in Cape May County. He'd even named it Whitesboro.

Mayme, like A'Lelia, was an aristocrat, the daughter of George Henry White, the last former slave to serve in Congress. An advocate for black education, by the turn of the twentieth century he was the only black member of Congress. A'Lelia and Mayme used to wonder what their parents would think, seeing them together, since the congressman and the tycoon had known each other through their work in the NAACP.

Like A'Lelia, Mayme sometimes found herself wanting. She just had no aspirations that matched her father's, as much as she loved being his daughter.

Mayme had heard his speeches repeated all through her childhood. The one she was proudest of, she could remember from heart. She would get breathless sometimes, picturing him on the floor of the Capitol, telling those men:

> It is easy for these gentlemen to taunt us with our inferiority, at the same time not mentioning the cause of this inferiority. It is rather hard to be accused of shiftlessness and idleness when the accuser closes the avenue of labor and industrial pursuits to us. It is hardly fair to accuse us of ignorance when it was made a crime under the former order of things to learn enough about letters to even read the word of God.[35]

In January 1901, he ended his career with an impassioned speech to Congress urging passage of a bill that would equate lynching with treason.

It was twenty-seven years before another black man was elected to Congress.

But Mayme had been glad to live in Philadelphia, where Father, who became a leading attorney and banker, built their prosperous lives. She would have lived there the rest of her life – if she hadn't met A'Lelia.

As their planned trip approached, A'Lelia decided that they'd forego Atlantic City and just go directly to a birthday party, in Long Branch, New Jersey, for their friend Mae Fain. They'd spend the whole weekend there. It was an ocean town, but it lacked gangsters, and that pleased A'Lelia.

All the warring gangster elements seemed to vacation in Atlantic City, as if it were Switzerland. A'Lelia knew that around the time of the Caspar Holstein kidnapping, Dutch Schultz had gone to Atlantic City for a gangster convention in the Ambassador, where he, Meyer Lansky, and Lucky Luciano had taken power from Al Capone.

She thought she'd be better off in Long Branch.

*   *   *

A'Lelia was too nervous to take the wheel, so Mayme drove all the way to the beach. There was no money for a driver.

When there were quiet spells in the car, A'Lelia kept having the oddest flashes of memory. She kept remembering her visits down to the Tuskegee Veterans Hospital, where her third husband, Dr. Kennedy, had worked. She had found herself lingering in the wards, particularly where the depressed men lay, trapped in their private hells. Now, in her daydreams, she kept seeing herself taking care of the men, washing them, talking to them, helping her husband to cure them. It would have been something palpable, nursing men to health.

Mae's party lasted the day. They waded in the ocean, flopped back into the surf. Mayme held A'Lelia's hand underwater, and for long stretches they floated on their backs in the shallows, eyes closed to the sun.

A lobster dinner. Champagne. A couple of pieces of chocolate cake, à la mode, vanilla melting into the dark icing-ribboned bit that remained on her plate.

"I'm sorry, Mae," A'Lelia said. "It's time for me to go to bed."

In the bedroom they shared, Mayme asked A'Lelia, "Baby, what's wrong?"

"I'm so glad you're here, Mayme. Look at me. I've had everything I wanted in life. I just didn't have it long enough."[36]

A'Lelia watched her friend get ready for bed and turn out the light. Pale moonlight came through the windows, illuminating Mayme as she walked closer.

A'Lelia's eyes welled with gratitude for Mayme's dear soul.

She made herself lie perfectly still so Mayme couldn't hear her crying. Enough of sorrowful A'Lelia. Let me be strong for tonight – for Mayme.

Mayme, come over here.
Please, Mayme.
Come closer.
Mmmmm.
I love you, Mayme.
I love you, Lelia.

It was after three in the morning when A'Lelia awakened with the pain of a spike splitting her head open.

"Mayme! Turn on the light! Mayme! I can't see!"

By morning, August 17, 1931, A'Lelia Walker was dead.

CHAPTER SEVENTEEN

Throngs of mourners crowded Seventh Avenue, swelling in every direction from the prominent funeral home. The doors to the chapel didn't open until the procession, which was late, finally arrived. Although the funeral was by invitation only, there was no room for hundreds who'd been asked to come. The turnout, of course, was as exuberant as it had always been for her parties.

Adam Clayton Powell, minister of Harlem's Abyssinian Baptist Church, stood over A'Lelia's coffin as the lucky mourners who had actually made it into the chapel took their seats. For a terribly long moment, he hovered in the soft light, watching the crowd. At the exact moment that a hush settled over the chapel, Powell said, "The Four Bon Tons will now sing."

The quartet, who'd performed on Broadway, in Harlem's swank nightclubs, and, most famously, at A'Lelia's mansion, came beside the casket and sang a Noël Coward number, "I'll See You Again."

Langston Hughes, who'd written a poem for the occasion, found the group's version of the song just perfect for the occasion. The Four Bon Tons "swung it lightly,"[37] he remembered.

As mourners clung to one another, the words softly echoed and carried out to Seventh Avenue: "just the echo of a sigh/goodbye . . ."

After an oratory that wove A'Lelia's life into the epic story of Madame Walker's rise to power, a member of A'Lelia's gay circle who'd appeared in *Porgy and Bess* read Langston's poem "To A'Lelia."

Mayme White held her face in her hands as she listened, but a deep wail escaped from her throat as Perry read the final lines of the poem:

> Let your prayers be as roses
> For this queen of the night.[38]

A'Lelia was buried at the Woodlawn Cemetery, in a plot beside beside her mother. The four hundred acres were vividly green, immense tombs and crypts polished, fresh flowers dotting the landscape.

In death, the Walkers were in the company of Mr. Woolworth, Mr Westinghouse, and Mr. Armour, and over the years they would find themselves joined by Miles Davis, Oscar Hammerstein II, and Joseph Stella, among others.

But on this Saturday, A'Lelia's casket, covered by twenty-four orchids, was lowered into the ground without a burial service.

Fairy Mae, her daughter, collapsed at the grave, limp, her hair splayed in two luscious pools beside her small head.

A'Lelia left half her estate to F. B. Ransom, and insisted in her will that he succeed her as the head of the Walker empire. She left the other half of her estate to Fairy Mae. The estate, which had been ravaged by expenses before A'Lelia's death, was over-generously estimated at around $1.2 million in the press – a last gesture of goodwill.

NOTES

1. As quoted in David Levering Lewis, *When Harlem Was in Vogue* (New York: Oxford University Press, 1989), p. 7.

2. From "Lament Over Love," in Langston Hughes, *The Collected Poems* (New York: Knopf, 1999), p. 45.

3. "Women Traders Going Back to Bridge Games; Say They Are Through with Stocks Forever," *New York Times*, October 30, 1929.

4. Lucille Bogan's "B.D. Women's Blues," as transcribed in Paul Oliver, *Blues Fell This Morning: Meaning in the Blues*, second edition (London: Cambridge University Press, 1990), p. 100.

5. The facts of this story are laid out in a letter of April 23, 1917, from A'Lelia Walker to Mr. Ransom, held at the Indiana Historical Society.

6. From "On Blanche Dunn," originally written for the Writer's Project of the WPA, collected in Thomas Wirth, ed., *Gay Rebel of the Harlem Renaissance: Selections from the Work of Richard Bruce Nugent* (Durham, NC: Duke University Press, 2002), pp. 220–21.

7. *Inter-State Tattler*, April 13, 1928, p. 11.

8. George Hannah's "Freakish Man Blues," as transcribed in Oliver, *Blues Fell This Morning*, p. 98.

9. "Jennie June" is a pseudonym (one of three) for the author of two memoirs I have taken great liberties with in the "Jennie June" chapters of this book. In some passages, I have tried to stay excruciatingly close to her genuine story; in others, I have elaborated at great length on her written record of her life story. Earl Lind, *Autobiography of an Androgyne* (New York: The Medico-Legal Journal, 1918). Earl Lind, *The Female Impersonators* (New York: The Medico-Legal Journal, 1922).

10. Anne Chisholm, *Nancy Cunard* (London: Sidgwick and Jackson, 1979), p. 183.

11. *National Police Gazette*, March 2, 1872.

12. As collected in Emory Holloway, ed., *The Uncollected Poetry and Prose of Walt Whitman*, volume 2 (Garden City, NY: Doubleday, Page & Company, 1921).

13. As quoted in Willard B. Gatewood, *Aristocrats of Color: The Black Elite 1880–1920* (Bloomington: Indiana University Press, 1993), p. 15.

14. *National Police Gazette*, December 17, 1864.

15. Abram Hill, "Dark Dame of Fortune." The Writer's Project of the WPA. October 11, 1939.

16. A'Lelia Bundles, *On Her Own Ground: The Life and Times of Madam C. J. Walker* (New York: Washington Square Press, 2001), p. 189.

17. As collected in Holloway, *The Uncollected Poetry and Prose of Walt Whitman*, volume 2.

18. As quoted in Timothy J. Gilfoyle, *City of Eros: New York City, Prostitution, and the Commercialization of Sex, 1790–1920* (New York: W.W. Norton, 1992), p. 210.

19. Wallace Thurman, *Infants of the Spring* (New York: Macaulay Company, 1932), p. 21. Nugent fictionalized, as noted in Wirth, *Gay Rebel of the Harlem Renaissance*.

20. As quoted in Wirth, *Gay Rebel of the Harlem Renaissance*, p. 82.

21. Richard Bruce Nugent. *Geisha Man*, in Wirth, *Gay Rebel of the Harlem Renaissance*.

22. Ibid.

23. Ibid.

24. Ibid.

25. Ibid.

26. Geraldyn Dismond, *Inter-State Tattler*, August 12, 1927.

27. Geraldyn Dismond, "Social Snapshots," *Inter-State Tattler*, February 22, 1929.

28. Osbert Sitwell, "New York in the Twenties," *Atlantic Monthly*, February 1962.

29. Bruce Kellner, ed., *Keep A-Inchin' Along: Selected Writings of Carl Van Vechten About Black Art and Letters (Contributions in Afro-American and African Studies)* (Westport, CT: Greenwood Publishing, 1979).

30. Interview in Lillian Faderman, *Odd Girls and Twilight Lovers: A History of Lesbian Life in Twentieth-Century America* (New York: Penguin, 1992).

31. A'Lelia Walker, letter to F. B. Ransom, September 13, 1915, Madame C. J. Walker Collection, Indiana Historical Society.

32. Countee Cullen and Hughes Allison, undated introduction to "The Sunny Side of the Street," an adaptation of the Leston Huntley–Natalie Johnson radio-serial, Countee Cullen Papers, Amistad Research Center, Tulane University.

33. Richard Bruce Nugent, "On the Dark Tower," originally written for the Writer's Project of the WPA, and collected in Wirth, *Gay Rebel of the Harlem Renaissance*.

34. As recounted in Steven Watson, *The Harlem Renaissance: Hub of African-American Culture, 1920–1930* (New York: Pantheon Books, 1995), pp. 143–144.

35. George Henry White, speech to Congress, February 23, 1900.

36. As quoted in Bundles, *On Her Own Ground*, p. 292.

37. Langston Hughes, *The Big Sea* (New York: Hill and Wang, 1940).

38. Langston Hughes, *Inter-State Tattler*, August 27, 1931.

SELECTED WORKS CONSULTED

In keeping with the *Urban Historicals* series mission – entertainment – I've taken great liberty in imagining dialogue, scenes, and memories of famous and obscure historical persons. Every named person in this book really lived – unnamed characters are based on composites or brief references, or they are imaginary.

Historical fiction, you might say. These are works that I found of particular use.

COVER DRAWINGS

Richard Bruce Nugent, from *Dance Magazine*, May 1928.

NEWSPAPERS

Inter-State Tattler. (Began in 1922 as *Hotel Tattler.*)

This Harlem weekly put a premium on distinctive voices in its gossip, society coverage, and thundering political editorials. A talent like Geraldyn Dismond, the paper's tireless socialite columnist, made the pages addictive, sparkling reading. I viewed the collection at the Schomburg Center for Research in Black Culture, in New York.

National Police Gazette.

This lurid tabloid covered sporting culture, crime, and changing social mores with tawdry aplomb. Frankly racist, vividly illustrated, with densely written articles in small print. A newspaper for readers, with the most provocatively illustrated details often buried in the thirtieth paragraph of a long piece.

Franklin, Donald E. "Black Adventurer Clamorgan Cut a Wide Swath in St. Louis; Even If He Was a Scoundrel, His Legacy Is Large." *St. Louis Dispatch.* February 28, 2001.

"Women Traders Going Back to Bridge Games; Say They Are Through with Stocks Forever." *New York Times.* October 30, 1929.

LETTERS

Jackman, Harold. Letters to Countee Cullen. Countee Cullen Papers, Amistad Research Center, Tulane University.

Walker, A'Lelia. Letters to Carl Van Vechten. James Weldon Johnson Papers, Beinecke Rare Book and Manuscript Library, Yale University.

Walker, A'Lelia. Letters to F. B. Ransom. Madame C.J. Walker Collection, Indiana Historical Society.

UNPUBLISHED PAPERS

Cullen, Countee, and Hughes Allison. Undated introduction to "The Sunny Side of the Street," an adaptation of the Leston Huntley–Natalie Johnson radio serial. Countee Cullen Papers, Amistad Research Center, Tulane University.

JOURNALS

Burroughs, William S. "The Last Words of Dutch Schultz." *The Atlantic Monthly,* volume 223, no. 6 (June 1969): 73–83.

Hill, Abram. "Dark Dame of Fortune." The Writer's Project of the WPA. October 11, 1939.

New York Press. Vices of a Big City; an expose of existing menaces to church and home in New York City. New York: J. E. Clark, c. 1890.

Nugent, Richard Bruce. "On the Dark Tower." The Writer's Project for the WPA. Undated. Microfiche from the Schomburg Center for Research in Black Culture, New York.

Powers, Peter. "'The Singing Man Who Must Be Reckoned With': Private Desire and Public Responsibility in the Poetry of Countee Cullen." *African American Review* 34:4 (Winter 2000): 661–678.

Weinberg, Jonathan. "Boy Crazy: Carl Van Vechten's Queer Collection." *The Yale Journal of Criticism* 7:2 (1991): 25–49.

BOOKS

Bankhead, Tallulah. *Tallulah.* New York: Harper & Brothers, 1952.

Bernard, Emily, ed. *Remember Me to Harlem: The Letters of Langston Hughes and Carl Van Vechten.* New York: Vintage, 2002.

Bundles, A'Lelia. *On Her Own Ground: The Life and Times of Madam C. J. Walker*. New York: Washington Square Press, 2001.

Rigorous, full-bodied, definitive biography of A'Lelia Walker's mother. With astonishing detail, and an intimate understanding of the Walker family's significance in American culture.

Chauncey, George. *Gay New York: Gender, Urban Culture, and the Making of the Gay Male World, 1890–1940*. New York: Basic Books, 1994.

A defiantly generous, addictively readable work of social history. Impeccable research: even the footnotes are compelling. I found hundreds of leads on new (to me) primary source material. Chauncey's arguments are so tight, you can't really argue with him. The definitive book on the subject.

Chisholm, Anne. *Nancy Cunard*. London: Sidgwick and Jackson, 1979.

Cohen, Patricia Cline. *The Murder of Helen Jewett: The Life and Death of a Prostitute in Nineteenth-Century New York*. New York: Knopf, 1998.

Coontz, Stephanie. *The Way We Never Were: American Families and the Nostalgia Trap*. New York: Basic Books, 1992.

An indispensible source of facts that undercut historical and political cliche.

Crockett, Davy. *A Narrative of the Life of David Crockett.* Lincoln, NE: University of Nebraska Press, 1987 (paperback reprint of 1834 original).

Douglas, Ann. *Terrible Honesty: Mongrel Manhattan in the 1920s.* New York: Farrar Straus & Giroux, 1995.

Faderman, Lillian. *Odd Girls and Twilight Lovers: A History of Lesbian Life in Twentieth-Century America.* New York: Penguin, 1992.

Ford, Charles Henri, and Parker Tyler. *The Young and Evil.* New York: Richard Kasak Books, 1988 (reprint edition).

Garber, Eric. "A Spectacle in Color: The Lesbian and Gay Subculture of Jazz Age Harlem." *Hidden from History: Reclaiming the Gay and Lesbian Past*, ed. Martin Duberman, Martha Vicinus, and George Chauncey, Jr. New York: New American Library, 1989. 318–331.

Gatewood, Willard B. *Aristocrats of Color: The Black Elite 1880–1920.* Bloomington: Indiana University Press, 1993.

Gilfoyle, Timothy J. *City of Eros: New York City, Prostitution, and the Commercialization of Sex, 1790–1920.* New York: W.W. Norton, 1992.

With nearly biblical authority and clarity, and absolutely no pandering, Gilfoyle illuminates the sexual evolution of commercial New York City.

Graham, Lawrence Otis. *Our Kind of People: Inside America's Black Upper Class.* New York: HarperCollins, 1999.

Gubar, Susan. *Racechanges: White Skin, Black Face in American Culture.* Oxford: Oxford University Press, 1997.

Harper, Frances E. W. *Iola Leroy, or Shadows Uplifted.* New York: Beacon Press, 1999 (reprint edition).

Holloway, Emory, ed. *The Uncollected Poetry and Prose of Walt Whitman,* volume 2. Garden City, NY: Doubleday, Page & Company, 1921.

Hughes, Langston. *The Collected Poems.* New York: Knopf, 1999.

———. *The Big Sea.* New York: Hill and Wang, 1940.

Johnson, James Weldon. *Black Manhattan.* New York: Da Capo Press, 1991 (reprint edition).

Kellner, Bruce. *Carl Van Vechten and the Irreverent Decades.* Norman, OK: The University of Oklahoma Press, 1968.

It's hard to be a white male from outside New York: writing about the Harlem Renaissance, and not experience sick-making twinges of embarrassment for this simultaneously serious and silly white promoter and exploiter of black culture – but the totality of his work, the collections and letters more than any of the writing itself, proves an indispensable historical record.

Kellner, Bruce, ed. *Letters of Carl Van Vechten*. New Haven: Yale University Press, 1997.

Lawrenson, Helen. *Stranger at the Party*. New York: Random House, 1972.

Lewis, David Levering. *W. E. B. Dubois: The Fight for Equality and the American Century, 1919–1963*. New York: Henry Holt, 2000.

Lewis, David Levering. *When Harlem Was in Vogue*. New York: Oxford University Press, 1989 (paperback edition).

Lind, Earl. *Autobiography of an Androgyne*. New York: The Medico-Legal Journal, 1918.

———. *The Female Impersonators*. New York: The Medico-Legal Journal, 1922.

I've made abundant use of the memoirs of this compelling figure. As the baby-doll fairy "Jennie June," Lind explored much of the New York underworld from the 1890s through at least the 1920s. The third volume of his memoirs, Riddle of the Underworld, *was never published, and after the publication of his second book, he disappeared from the public record.*

Lind is a prominent source in George Chauncey's landmark Gay New York. *I tend to see his memoirs as a darker record* of homosexual life in the 1890s than Chauncey does, but that is a tribute to the texts' disturbing complexities. His voice is so distinctive that I've tried to make as few alterations to his actual memoirs as possible. All of his memories of the 1890s are presented in his exact words with some minor alterations (tense, point of view) in service of my story. "Jennie June," as far as I know, was not at the Manhattan Casino for the 1930 Faggots Ball, and her dialogue and memories are a mix of genuine text from Lind's memoirs and my own invention.

Marks, Carole, and Diana Edkins. *The Power of Pride: Style-makers and Rulebreakers of the Harlem Renaissance*. New York: Crown, 1999.

The most lavishly illustrated book on the Harlem Renaissance.

Mitchell, Donald G. *Reveries of a Bachelor*. New York: R. F. Fenno & Co., 1906 (reprint).

Niles, Blair. *Strange Brother*. London: GMP, 1991.

Oliver, Paul. *Blues Fell This Morning: Meaning in the Blues*. London: Cambridge University Press, 1990 (second edition).

Excellent source of lyrics to rare and out-of-print blues songs.

Sante, Luc. *Low Life*. New York: Vintage, 1992.

Schoener, Allon. *Harlem on My Mind*. New York: The New Press, 1995 (paperback reprint).

Smith-Rosenberg, Carroll. *Disorderly Conduct: Visions of Gender in Victorian America*. New York: Oxford University Press, 1986 (paperback reprint).

Van Vechten, Carl. *Nigger Heaven*. Urbana: University of Illinois Press, 2000.

Watson, Steven, *The Harlem Renaissance: Hub of African-American Culture, 1920–1930*. New York: Pantheon Books, 1995.

Such an ingenious cultural encyclopedia, abundantly illustrated, compact, and with a collector's eye for the telling quote, the choice slang, the surprising anecdote.

Whitman, Walt. *Leaves of Grass*. Edited by Sculley Bradley and Harold W. Blodgett. New York: W. W. Norton, 1973.

During Jennie June's feverish reveries, she recalls fragments of Whitman's poetry.

Wirth, Thomas, ed., *Gay Rebel of the Harlem Renaissance: Selections from the Work of Richard Bruce Nugent*. Durham, NC: Duke University Press, 2002.

Wirth brings the Harlem Renaissance's most beguiling presence to life, saves his art from obscurity, and does it all with warmth and rigor.

ACKNOWLEDGMENTS

Thanks to Colin Dickerman, Joel Rose, Thomas Wirth, Greg Villepique, the Schomburg Center, the Amistad Center at Tulane, the New York Historical Society, the Indiana Historical Society, the New York Public Library, Amanda Brunholzl, Betsy Berne, Amanda Filipacchi, Ken Foster, Sloan Harris, Heather Byer, and my family for all their support.

A NOTE ON THE TYPE

The text of this book is set in Linotype Goudy Old Style. It was designed by Frederic Goudy (1865–1947), an American designer whose types were very popular during his lifetime, and particularly fashionable in the 1940s. He was also a craftsman who cut the metal patterns for his type designs, engraved matrices, and cast type.

The design for Goudy Old Style is based on Goudy Roman, with which it shares a "hand-wrought" appearance and asymmetrical serifs, but unlike Goudy Roman its capitals are modeled on Renaissance lettering.

APR 2 9 2003